Transliteracy in Complex Information Environments

CHANDOS
INFORMATION PROFESSIONAL SERIES
Series Editor: Ruth Rikowski
(email: Rikowskigr@aol.com)

Chandos' new series of books is aimed at the busy information professional. They have been specially commissioned to provide the reader with an authoritative view of current thinking. They are designed to provide easy-to-read and (most importantly) practical coverage of topics that are of interest to librarians and other information professionals. If you would like a full listing of current and forthcoming titles, please visit www.chandospublishing.com.

New authors: we are always pleased to receive ideas for new titles; if you would like to write a book for Chandos, please contact Dr Glyn Jones on g.jones.2@elsevier.com or telephone +44 (0) 1865 843000.

Transliteracy in Complex Information Environments

Suzana Sukovic

AMSTERDAM • BOSTON • HEIDELBERG • LONDON
NEW YORK • OXFORD • PARIS • SAN DIEGO
SAN FRANCISCO • SINGAPORE • SYDNEY • TOKYO
Chandos Publishing is an imprint of Elsevier

Chandos Publishing is an imprint of Elsevier
50 Hampshire Street, 5th Floor, Cambridge, MA 02139, United States
The Boulevard, Langford Lane, Kidlington, OX5 1GB, United Kingdom

British Library Cataloguing-in-Publication Data
A catalogue record for this book is available from the British Library

Library of Congress Cataloging-in-Publication Data
A catalog record for this book is available from the Library of Congress

ISBN: 978-0-08-100875-1 (print)
ISBN: 978-0-08-100901-7 (online)

For information on all Chandos Publishing
visit our website at https://www.elsevier.com

Working together
to grow libraries in
developing countries

www.elsevier.com • www.bookaid.org

Publisher: Glyn Jones
Acquisition Editor: George Knott
Editorial Project Manager: Tessa De Roo
Production Project Manager: Omer Mukthar
Cover Designer: Mark Rogers

Typeset by MPS Limited, Chennai, India

That which your hands
Have touched
Has since perished.
Slowly the fire of life
Turns all that lives to black dust.
However, all that your heart
Has touched
And cherished
Has survived. Only love
Lives longer than us.

By Olga Chugai (1944–2015), translated from Russian by Philip Nikolayev

Contents

Biography

Dr Suzana Sukovic is a librarian, researcher, and educator with extensive professional experience in the information industry, mainly in the academic sector. She has also worked in academic teaching and research roles. She has completed a number of innovative projects, including applications of technology in research, teaching, and learning. Dr Sukovic has published papers on issues related to technology in scholarly research, and on innovation and creativity in libraries. Her doctoral thesis explored roles of electronic texts in research projects in the humanities. Transliteracy, learning and knowledge creation, and library innovation are her main professional and research interests.

Affiliations and Expertise

Executive Director Educational Research and Evidence Based Practice, HETI (Health Education and Training Institute)

Transliteracy; technology in learning and knowledge production; adult education; library creativity and innovation

Transliteracy in Complex Information Environments considers this relatively new concept, which has attracted a great deal of interest in the library and information field, particularly among practitioners.

The notion of transliteracy arises in the context of increasingly complex information and communication environments characterized by multimodality and new roles for creators and consumers.

Transliteracy concerns the ability to apply and transfer a range of skills and contextual insights to a variety of settings. Rather than focusing on any one skillset or technology, transliteracy is about fluidity of movement across a range of contexts.

This book is concerned with processes of learning and knowledge creation. An understanding of transliteracy emerges from research data gathered in university and high school settings. Transliteracy is considered in relation to other literacies as an overarching framework. Applications in education and lifelong learning are discussed. Social aspects of transliteracy are considered in relation to academic cultures and broader social trends, particularly hybrid cultures.

Readership: Professionals, academics, and tertiary students, within information and library studies, education, and communication.

Acknowledgments

During the preparation of this book, I benefited from generous contributions and the support of many people. First of all, I am grateful to everyone who contributed to my research. Academics, teachers, and the team on the project *A History of Aboriginal Sydney* shared with me their experiences and insightful reflections. Vinnies girls, as students of St. Vincent's College are known, shared their stories, thoughts and, above all, joy of learning. This book would not be possible without them. Teachers Julia Hegarty and Cheryl McArthur worked with me on integrating transliteracy in the classroom. A librarian, Alycia Bailey, gave me permission to use data from her transliteracy project, LevelUp. Working with them was my privilege.

Many people from St. Vincent's College supported me during my work on transliteracy. I am grateful to the College Executive team—my work would be impossible without their support. My special thanks are due to Robert Graham, Director of Teaching and Learning, with whom I often discussed integration of transliteracy in education. The Heads of Departments team contributed to curriculum mapping projects and generously provided their feedback in many after-school meetings. My special thanks are due to the library staff who presented transliteracy workshops with me, took ethnographic notes, and gave me valuable feedback and support.

I wish to acknowledge a research grant from the Australian Library and Information Association, which provided funding for a 2013 research trip to investigate transliteracy. During this trip I met with Dr Sue Thomas, who also invited a few members of the initial Transliteracy Group. Our conversation and Dr Thomas's reflection about the development of transliteracy provided me with the context and gave me a sense of how my work could make a contribution. Two beautiful booklets related to the inception of transliteracy, which Dr Thomas gave me in our meeting, were on my desk as I was writing this book.

I am grateful to Professor Joyce Kirk, who generously offered to read my manuscript and provided me with very helpful feedback. I have benefited greatly from her input. Anonymous reviewers of my book proposal also made some valuable suggestions. Thank you to Tessa de Roo and George Knott from Elsevier for their expert guidance through the book publishing process and to Cindy Minor for all her support.

Zoran Malesevic applied his transliteracy skills to translate my ideas and early sketches into graphical representations of the transliteracy conceptual model and transliteracy palettes. Zoran and our son, Milan, have been my closest companions and best supporters on this journey.

Parts of my book drew upon my published articles. These instances are acknowledged in references. Section 4.4, Transliterate Reading and Writing, was taken from my paper "Transliterate reading", published in 2015 in Scholar.Res.Commun. 6.

Introduction

1

1991. Before I climb out of the car in front of my house, I am putting the thick volume of Gregory's Street Directory into the glove compartment. It's been a challenging drive to a meeting on the other side of Sydney. Now I am opening my mailbox with anticipation and I am not disappointed. My heart skips a bit when I see my name in a friend's handwriting. Even better is a firm envelope which, I know, contains an audiotape from my family overseas. Letters are never long enough for us. Before I go to the kitchen to start cooking dinner, I take out the newspaper I bought this morning and switch on my computer, plug the cord into the modem, and wait for the happy sound of connection. My private email is on my home computer. I am wondering about the continuation of a discussion on a mailing list I am following. When I finish with email, I'll call a friend at work. Maybe I should get two phone lines—one for the phone, another for the Internet.

2016. Before I climb out of the car in front of my house, I switch off the GPS navigator on my phone. It's been a long drive to a meeting on the other side of Sydney. I wish the voice navigation would give me more advance notice and I thought the route was a strange choice, but the drive was uneventful otherwise. I am passing by the mailbox I last checked two days ago. If there is a bill, it can wait another day. Before I go to the kitchen to start cooking dinner, I take out Wordly, *the school literary magazine. I smile in anticipation of reading the students' clever writing, but also thinking how they keep ignoring me when I try to raise the possibility of an electronic magazine. Between the stages of cooking, I check my work mail on my phone and catch up with Twitter. Facebook feed never ceases to amuse me—economic analysis, pictures of a friend's baby, wise sayings on colored background, a petition to help refugees, and a video of a cat running away from a mouse. My musing is interrupted by the insistent sound of a Skype call. My heart skips a bit when I see it's my niece calling from the airport in Singapore.*

Our information and communication environment has changed enormously in the last 25 years. We all know the amount of information that surrounds us is staggering, but the numbers still come as a surprise to most of us. The global memory stored in technology "has roughly doubled every 3 years over recent decades, from less than 3 exabytes in 1986 to about 300 in 2007. Had we chosen to store this on double printed book paper, we could have covered every square centimetre of the world's landmasses with one sheet of paper in 1986, with one layer of books by 2007, and by 2010 with two layers of books" (Hilbert, 2012, p. 9). However, as Hilbert points out, the content has not changed that much—text and images still dominate our information world.

The predictions of a paperless office have not eventuated. Expectations that children born after 2000 would be completely immersed in digital worlds have not been realized either. It is highly unlikely that books, pen, and paper will disappear any time soon. Analog technologies have their distinct advantages, but we also remain physical beings with minds embedded in our well-wired bodies. A human

Transliteracy in Complex Information Environments. DOI: http://dx.doi.org/10.1016/B978-0-08-100875-1.00001-7

body has "an informational capacity that is roughly in the same order-of-magnitude ballpark as all of our technological devices put together" (Hilbert, 2012, p. 12). While digital technologies are developing at an unprecedented rate, changing our daily lives, our experiences are still embodied; not to mention that the entirety of our cultural memory cannot be digitized—not as long as we are human beings as we are now.

This book is about the transition in which we live rich digital lives but remain connected with information contained in our physical environment and analog technologies. Thinking about transliteracy includes different abilities and skill sets, but transliteracy is mainly about movement across a whole range of contexts, technologies, and modalities. This is something people have always done, but modern technologies have brought different areas of our lives closer together and amplified the complexities of moving across them. Our work and home lives are often separated by a click on a browser tab. As you are reading this, on screen or paper, there may be a screen within easy reach with browser tabs for your email, Twitter feed, a magazine article, and the latest search for the best price of a product you want to buy. On your phone is a message from your family member or a friend, and in the background you can hear streamed music and a soft hum of traffic. Maybe you respond simultaneously in different languages. Investigations of transliteracy are concerned with the fluency of our movement across this complex information field we experience daily. How do we think and what do we experience as we move across it? What are the skills we need? Does it affect our social interactions? Before considering transliteracy further, it needs to be situated among other literacies that we use to understand our fast-changing information world.

1.1 Literacies landscape

The understanding that information and technologies which enable it are at the core of a productive life is the basis of UNESCO's resolution to accept the International Federation of Library Associations and Institutions (IFLA) Media and Information Literacy Recommendations. An important aspect of the resolution is the recognition "that the achievement of UNESCO's vision of knowledge societies is dependent on moving beyond information and communication technology (ICT) infrastructure and access toward building the capacity of all citizens to participate actively and effectively in emerging knowledge societies" (UNESCO, 2014, p. 50).

Media and information literacy. UNESCO saw media and information literacy (MIL) as "essential for lifelong learning" and "a prerequisite for sustainable development," recognizing MIL as "a means for achieving the goal of universal and equitable access to information and knowledge" (UNESCO, 2014, p. 50). MIL brings together two traditionally separate fields, encompassing a range of related literacies. "MIL is concerned with the ability to access the media [new and old] and other information sources, to understand and evaluate critically their contents and functions and to critically use them to create communications in a variety of contexts including teaching and learning, self-expression, creativity and civic participation" (UNESCO, 2013, p. 175). A number of detailed documents developed by UNESCO to promote MIL show a broad approach to developing information capacities, encompassing many of the new literacies identified in the last couple of decades.

Stordy (2015) considered a taxonomy of literacies and pointed out that the term "literacy," in existence since the end of the 19th century, came into prominence in education in the 1970s, with regards to reading and writing as meaning-making activities. In the 1980s, subject literacies were discussed, while new literacies took the center stage with the rise of digital technologies. Stordy referred to work by Lankshear and Knobel in pointing out "paradigm cases" of new literacies. These new literacies (e.g., Internet, cyber-, information literacy, MIL) tend to be participatory, collaborative, and distributed.

Multiliteracies emerged as an influential concept from a meeting of the New London Group in 1996. The members chose the term to capture two important arguments they had with "the emerging cultural, institutional, and global order: the multiplicity of communication channels and media, and the increasing saliency of cultural and linguistic diversity" (Cazden et al., 1996, p. 63). Their focus was on "the increasing multiplicity and integration of significant modes of meaning-making, where the textual is also related to the visual, the audio, the spatial, the behavioural, and so on" (p. 64). The concept of multiliteracies gained some prominence in education, especially as it was related to multiple intelligences, a well-spread educational concept. Tyner (1998) pointed out that the connection between multiliteracy and Gardner's multiple intelligences became a problem of oversimplification for both.

Digital literacy is one of the key new literacies focusing on a capacity to effectively work with digital technology. "It is the ability to make and share meaning in different modes and formats; to create, collaborate and communicate effectively and to understand how and when digital technologies can best be used to support these processes" (Hague and Payton, 2010, p. 4). Education is often concerned with the development of digital literacy as an addition to traditional literacies of reading and writing. Digital fluency is a closely related concept developed for teaching and learning in schools and framed as a skill set for the 21st century (White, 2013).

Information literacy is probably the most prominent of the new literacies. It was identified in the 1980s before most other new literacies and developed as the literacy for the information age. There are currently a number of models and frameworks in use (Bundy, 2004; Bruce et al., 2006; SCONUL, 2011), most of them sharing key aspects.

While information literacy has had a wide application in educational contexts, it has been criticized for simplistic approaches. Lloyd (2010) pointed out the complexity of the concept and its narrow application to formal education and individual learning with limited consideration for work and collaborative practices.

Limberg et al. (2012) considered different theoretical approaches and discussed the interdependence of information literacy and its context. They found that the term "information literacies," in the plural, would be more suited to reflecting the complexity of information literacy. A view of information literacy as flexible and contextual was also emphasized through the concept of information literacy frames (Bruce et al., 2006; Lupton, 2008).

The ACRL information literacy model and its recent changes have been indicative of some of the discussions about the value of information literacy and the need for its development. ACRL (Association of College and Research Libraries, a division of the Americal Library Association) defined information literacy as "a set of abilities requiring individuals to 'recognize when information is needed and have the ability to locate, evaluate, and use effectively the needed information'" (ACRL, 2000, p. 2). This definition refers to the previous ACRL Report (1989). IT skills are seen as intertwined with, but separate from information literacy: "Information literacy initiates, sustains, and extends lifelong learning through abilities which may use technologies but are ultimately independent of them" (ACRL, 2000, p. 3). This model of information literacy is reflected in ACRL's 5 standards and 22 performance indicators. Standards relate to the ability of an information-literate person to do the following:

- *Determine the extent of information needed*
- *Access the needed information effectively and efficiently*
- *Evaluate information and its sources critically*
- *Incorporate selected information into one's knowledge base*
- *Use information effectively to accomplish a specific purpose*
- *Understand the economic, legal, and social issues surrounding the use of information, and access and use information ethically and legally*

ACRL (2000, pp. 2–3)

The ACRL's information literacy framework has been radically revised recently to include social aspects: "Information literacy is the set of integrated abilities encompassing the reflective discovery of information, the understanding of how information is produced and valued, and the use of information in creating new knowledge and participating ethically in communities of learning" (ACRL, 2016, p. 3). The new framework is underpinned by the idea of threshold concepts, described as ideas and processes in any discipline, which are so deeply ingrained that they go unnoticed by practitioners (Hofer et al., 2012). It is based on the following six concepts:

- *Authority Is Constructed and Contextual*
- *Information Creation as a Process*
- *Information Has Value*
- *Research as Inquiry*
- *Scholarship as Conversation*
- *Searching as Strategic Exploration*

ACRL (2016, p. 3)

The new framework has opened vigorous discussions and invited both positive responses and strong criticism, especially in the United States (Saracevic, 2014; Bellin, 2015). Arguments for the continuity of the previous, well-known information literacy framework and impetus for change both indicate the relevance and the complexities of information literacy. In June 2016, the ACRL Board of Directors decided to rescind the previous standards, so only the latest version is currently supported.

Metaliteracy is the most recent of the new literacies. It emphasizes self-reflection: "To be metaliterate requires individuals to understand their existing literacy strengths and areas for improvement and make decisions about their learning. The ability to critically self-assess different competencies and to recognize one's need for integrated literacies in today's information environments is a metaliteracy" (Mackey and Jacobson, 2014, p. 2). Metaliteracy is positioned as a key element in the new information literacy framework. Its focus on self-reflection and self-assessment, especially in relation to a range of literacies, is certainly relevant in everyday information practice, but how exactly it could be developed remains unclear at this point.

Application of new literacies. New literacies capture many of the complexities of living, learning, and working in the contemporary information world, pointing toward a need to develop a broad base of skills, abilities, and knowledge. Preparedness for living in developed information environments will become even more important in the future, considering the predictions of further acceleration in information growth, development of digital technologies, and fast workplace changes, following which the current young generations will work in jobs that do not exist today and have several careers during their working lives. Considering this, information and technological skills should be the top priority of education. The reality is, however, far from it. There is hardly another so important a skill set developed in a more haphazard way in many schools and universities, and it is usually treated on a "need to know" basis in professional settings.

There are several reasons for the neglect of the systematic development of information and technological skills. One is that formal education, especially on secondary and tertiary levels, is subject- and discipline-based. The nature and complexity of living in today's information environment is dictated by the fact that it is not confined to subjects and educational categories, and that information skills can be taught only in limited ways within strict disciplinary boundaries. While disciplinary knowledge is important and relevant, it cannot support the development of cross-disciplinary skills and types of lateral thinking required in working with information in real life.

Another reason is the idea that young people, simply through their upbringing, are now prepared to work with new technologies. Until the age of five, most millennials in Western countries and large parts of the world watched television and used TV sets, handled various digital devices, and played computer games. It is easy to assume that digital technologies are their natural environment. What is often forgotten is that these children normally used pens, paper, and books as well, but no one expects them to be inherently skilled at reading, writing, and drawing. The abilities of handling a device and of intellectually processing the content it gives access to are vastly different skills. The notion of a "digital native" has been thoroughly studied and confirmed as a myth (Miller, 2012; Cooper et al., 2013; Hinrichsen and Coombs, 2013; Smith et al., 2013; boyd, 2014; Lehmans and Cordier, 2014). Students struggle with information skills and basic understanding of how computers and the digital world work. That they are not taught systematically may be based on an assumption that they know more than their teachers, but there is also no clear requirement to include these skills in the curriculum and the assessment of student learning. boyd (2014) wrote that "digital natives" is a dangerous notion as it justifies the exclusion of key skills from formal teaching.

Finally, new literacies are presented as a range of similar, yet different skill sets, which makes them difficult to integrate in the classroom and in professional learning, especially in addition to all the other demands. Even the most willing educators and leaders of professional development are often confused and discouraged by many different options, especially in the absence of clear requirements. Before embarking on an investigation of transliteracy, it is important to clarify that transliteracy will not be offered as another option on the smorgasbord of literacies. As Mackey and Jacobson (2014, p. 19) noted, "transliteracy provides a unified approach to literacy, rather than developing a new discrete literacy every time a new technology emerges." Transliteracy will be considered as a framework to work within a given context with existing and new skill sets, technologies, and approaches.

1.2   Transliteracy: origins and development

Transliteracy as a concept originated in the work of academics who were involved in some digital building and tinkering, people who got their hands dirty with some practical work. And that is the essence of transliteracy—it is not only an abstract idea but also an embodied practice and sensory experience. As the very notion of transliteracy suggests, it is neither an idea or a practice: it is both. The name originates from the word "transliterate," meaning to convert from one script to another (e.g., transliteration of a word from the Greek to the Latin alphabet). The concept originated in Alan Liu's *Transliteracies Project* initiated at the University of California in 2005 as an investigation of practices of online reading. A few years after its commencement, the group involved with the Transliteracies Project (Liu, s. a., RoSE Prospectus) wrote:

> *Several years of work now leads Transliteracies to focus on a specific, high-value research-and-development direction—one that positions online reading as a new kind of research activity positioned in a **sweet spot between academic and mainstream information practices**.*
>
> *Emphasis by SS*

That "sweet spot between" remains the position of transliteracy. The concept was adopted and taken in a new direction by Sue Thomas and the Production and Research in Transliteracy (PART) group at the Institute of Creative Technologies at De Montfort University. The ideas, however, stayed in the space "between." The PART group consisted of academics, media producers, and writers of electronic literature with insights into theoretical thinking and experiences from media practice. In their paper, *Transliteracy: Crossing Divides* (Thomas et al., 2007), the authors introduced transliteracy as a concept which captures dynamic relationships between different types of literacies, technologies, and social and cultural contexts. Transliteracy was defined as "the ability to read, write and interact across a range of platforms, tools and media from signing and orality through handwriting, print, TV, radio and film, to digital social networks" (Thomas et al., 2007, What is Transliteracy? para 1). In discussing the origins of the concept, the authors wrote:

> The concept of media ecology developed by McLuhan, Ong, Postman and others is certainly closely related to transliteracy. The difference lies in transliteracy's insistence upon a lateral approach to history, context and culture, its interest in lived experience, and its focus on interpretation via practice and production. It is characteristic of our deliberations that we do not view digital media as part of a linear historical progression, but see them as manifestations of other similar modes of communication. In our view, the ecology of transliteracy is both global and historical.
>
> Thomas et al. (2007, Tracing Transliteracy, para 2)

The key aspect of transliteracy is "fluidity of movement across the field—between a range of contexts, modalities, technologies and genres" (Sukovic, 2014, p. 207). As Ipri (2010, p. 532) pointed out, "transliteracy is concerned with mapping meaning across different media and not about developing particular literacies about various media." It can also "capture the construction, use, and movement of texts across communicative and geographical spaces" (Hull et al., 2010, p. 87). While transliteracy has a broad and encompassing approach, it remains subjective and grounded in personal experience.

The concept has been enthusiastically received by librarians who recognized that transliteracy captures much of the experience of their daily work with clients. The library and information profession deals on a practical and theoretical level with the idea of a broad, encompassing information world, filtered through individual sense-making. Transliteracy emerged as a natural fit for librarians' ways of thinking. Insights based on hands-on practice allowed librarians to recognize the quality that distinguished transliteracy from other similar concepts. As Thomas et al. noted, the "'patterned ways' of transliteracy are multiple, varied, and often physical. A sense of how it feels to hold a feather quill, chisel a stone, type on a keyboard, or take a photograph, is important and helps connect the material product—a letter, photo, etc.—to the means of production" (Thomas et al., 2007, Going Across and Beyond, para 3). Librarians' knowledge and lived experience enabled instant connection with the idea of transliteracy.

In the years following publication of the article by the PART group, transliteracy has been embedded in many and varied library projects, and it has triggered lively online discussions and active online promotion. School and law librarians alike saw how transliteracy related to their users and how it could be applied to enhance library and information services. The Transliteracy Research Group Archive 2006–2013 (2013) curates a significant part of this activity and the embedding of transliteracy in library and information programs continues as the idea takes roots in practice. Stordy (2015, p. 470) sees transliteracy as part of the ideological-paradigm perspective, which focuses on "fundamentally new social practices" which "come about because of new technologies."

There is a noticeable gap between the high levels of interest in transliteracy among the library and allied professions and the scarcity of research-based writing about the concept. A group of scholars from the University of Bordeaux researched transliteracy in the school context and in relation to the education of teacher librarians (Cordier and Lehmans, 2012; Liquete, 2012; Lehmans and Cordier, 2014; Lehmans and Mazurier, 2015). Their work will be considered in Chapter 4, Transliteracy in Practice, to explore transliteracy and learning. A study into transliteracy and digital storytelling (Sukovic, 2014) is also situated in a school context. Thomas (2013) conducted a study into the connection between transliteracy and creativity, and Megwalu (2014, 2015) related examples from the practice of a reference librarian to transliteracy. While these studies provide valuable insights, there is significant scope for further research-based investigations of transliteracy.

1.3   About this book

Transliteracy is an ability to use diverse analog and digital technologies, techniques, modes, and protocols to search for and work with a variety of resources; to collaborate and participate in social networks; and to communicate meanings and new knowledge by using different tones, genres, modalities, and media. Transliteracy consists of skills, knowledge, thinking, and acting, which enable fluid "movement across" in a way that is defined by situational, social, cultural, and technological contexts.

This work arises from many years of my professional and academic experience in the library and information field. I am saying "professional and academic" as a communication aid, but for me they are not separate. This book is firmly situated in a "sweet spot between academic and mainstream information practices" (Liu, s.a., RoSE Prospectus). It considers transliteracy as it emerges from research data gathered in university- and practice-based projects, and connects it with studies and theories in a broader field. The definition of transliteracy above arises from data analysis.

This book is concerned with processes of learning and knowledge production. It is another separation to aid communication, but the difference between learning and knowledge production is only a matter of degree. Because, what are scholarly work and knowledge production if not forms of learning? The focus on learning and knowledge creation is significant, as they are a prime indicator of changes in the way we think and develop ideas.

"We need ethnographies of transliteracy, studies of its social, cultural, and power relationships and of its networked vernacular from the perspectives of those who live and work within it" (Thomas et al., 2007, Everyday Life in a Transliterate World, para 2). The transliteracy study presented here is based on data gathered from teenagers in high school and humanities scholars in university settings. They provided insights into what I see as a transliteracy range on a learning continuum from young teenagers to senior academics. Data was gathered also from teachers and research teams to deepen the sense of what is happening with transliteracy in lived experiences. This book is a contribution to the closing of the gap between the need to understand the complexity of "moving across" information domains and the scarcity of research-based evidence. It is also a prolonged moment of lingering in the space between theory and practice.

1.3.1 Book overview

After this introductory chapter, there are five chapters in this book.

Chapter 2. Study of Transliteracy: Approach considers projects on which my transliteracy study is based. The methodological approach is outlined and project details are provided to enhance readers' understanding of the context and assist colleagues in carrying out similar projects in their workplaces.

Chapter 3. Exploring Transliteracy grounds an understanding of transliteracy in the research data. It presents the conceptual model of transliteracy and explores complex practices and meanings uncovered during the study. The definition of transliteracy provided above and in the chapter is based on research findings, providing a solid basis for evidence-based understanding of the concept.

Chapter 4. Transliteracy in Practice considers aids and challenges to transliteracy and then focuses on implementation of transliteracy in teaching and learning. A transliteracy framework for formal and informal education on all levels and a model of transliteracy palettes are presented in the chapter. Pedagogies for transliteracy and the complexities of reading and writing with different technologies are also discussed.

Chapter 5. Transliterate Cultures starts by focusing on academic cultures. *Living in the city of villages* is proposed as a theory of how academics negotiate academic cultures, personal research interests, and the demands of scholarly work. The second part of the chapter considers transliteracy in relation to global social trends and hybrid cultures.

Chapter 6. Implications for the Library and Information Field discusses applications of transliteracy in information theory and practice. It outlines how the library and information field can contribute to and support transliterate practices.

Being a book about "moving across," it crosses several disciplinary territories. It is of interest to professionals, academics, and students primarily in the library and information field, and also in education and social sciences, as they seek to understand changes in the way we think, learn, and produce knowledge. As far I am aware, this is the first book on transliteracy.

Glossary of words used in this book

Digital story A short story prepared on computer which integrates text, sound (voiceover and music), and a series of still images; very short video clips can be used as well.

Format File format in computing; particular recognizable style and structure in mass media production.

Genre A literary genre is a particular category of work using common conventions which make it easily recognizable by readers or audience. It can relate to literary mode (lyric, narrative, dramatic), or type of subject matter (crime, biography); a category of composition (e.g., poetry, fiction), or formal structure (e.g., types of poetry or novel).

Media Materials, methods, or technical processes used in art or communication. The word has many different meanings. In this book, it usually refers to media such as print, film, television, and radio.

Modality This has different meanings, depending on the discipline. In this book, it refers to channels of sensory perception (e.g., vision, hearing). Modality denotes mode, or manner.

Stop motion A series of pictures which are played in succession to create an impression of movement.

Tone The mood or atmosphere of a work. It can refer to the author's attitude to the reader (e.g., formal, intimate, pompous) or to the type of delivery (e.g., ironic, light, sentimental).

Voice Refers to the tone, style, and personality through which a story or ideas are presented. It refers to speech patterns as well as to the content (e.g., an authoritative academic voice, the narrative voice of a storyteller, voices of the public who tell their stories, an individual writer's voice).

Most entries are based on the *Oxford Dictionary of Literary Terms* (Oxford University Press) and *A Dictionary of Media and Communication* (Chandler et al., 2011).

References

ACRL, 1989. Presidential Committee on Information Literacy: Final Report. Association of College and Research Libraries, Washington, DC.

ACRL, 2000. Information Literacy Competency Standards for Higher Education. Association of College and Research Libraries, Chicago, IL.

ACRL, 2016. Framework for Information Literacy for Higher Education. Association of College and Research Libraries, Chicago, IL.

Bellin, I., 2015. Beyond the threshold: conformity, resistance, and the ACRL Information Literacy Framework for Higher Education. Throwback Thursday. Available from: http://www.inthelibrarywiththeleadpipe.org/2015/beyond-the-threshold-conformity-resistance-and-the-aclr-information-literacy-framework-for-higher-education/ (accessed 17.06.16.).

boyd, D., 2014. It's Complicated: the Social Lives of Networked Teens. Yale University Press, New Haven.

Bruce, C., Edwards, S., Lupton, M., 2006. Six frames for information literacy education: a conceptual framework for interpreting the relationships between theory and practice. Italics5.

Bundy, A. (Ed.), 2004. Australia and New Zealand Information Literacy Framework. Australian and New Zealand Institute for Information Literacy, Adelaide.

Cazden, C., Cope, B., Fairclough, N., Gee, J., Kalantzis, M., Kress, G., et al., 1996. A pedagogy for multiliteracies: designing social futures. Harvard Educ. Rev. 66, 60–92.

Chandler, D., Munday, R., Oxford University Press, 2011. A dictionary of media and communication, Oxford Paperback Reference. 1st ed. Oxford University Press, Oxford, New York.

Cooper, N., Lockyer, L., Brown, I., 2013. Developing multiliteracies in a technology-mediated environment. Educ. Media Int. 50, 93–107.

Cordier, A., Lehmans, A., 2012. Distance learning as a central issue for the learning and professionalization process of professeurs documentalistes: the French synthesis of transliteracy. School Libraries Worldwide. 18, 41–50.

Hague, C., Payton, S., 2010. Digital Literacy Across the Curriculum (Futurelab Handbook). Futurelab, Bristol.

Hilbert, M., 2012. How much information is there in the "information society"? Significance. 9, 8–12.

Hinrichsen, J., Coombs, A., 2013. The five resources of critical digital literacy: a framework for curriculum integration. Res. Learn. Technol. 21.

Hofer, A.R., Townsend, L., Brunetti, K., 2012. Troublesome Concepts and Information Literacy: Investigating Threshold Concepts for IL Instruction. Libraries & The Academy.

Hull, G.A., Stornaiuolo, A., Sahni, U., 2010. Cultural citizenship and cosmopolitan practice: global youth communication online. English Educ. 42, 331–367.

Ipri, T., 2010. Introducing transliteracy: what does it mean to academic libraries? College Res. Librar News. 71, 532–533, 567.

Lehmans, A., Cordier, A., 2014. Transliteracy and knowledge formats. In: Kurbanoglu, S., Spiranec, S., Grassian, E., Mizrachi, D., Catts, R. (Eds.), Information Literacy: Lifelong Learning and Digital Citizenship in the 21st Century; Second European Conference, ECIL 2014. Springer, Dubrovnik, Croatia.

Lehmans, A., Mazurier, V., 2015. Transfer, transformation, transition: what the school librarian can do in transliteracy, the French context. In: Das, L., Brand-Gruwel, S., Kok, K., Walhout, J. (Eds.), The School Library Rocks: Living it, Learning it, Loving it, 44th International Association of School Librarianship International Conference, Incorporating the 19th International Forum on Research in School Librarianship. International Association of School Librarianship, Maastricht, Netherlands.

Limberg, L., Sundin, O., Talja, S., 2012. Three theoretical perspectives on information literacy. Human IT. 11, 93–130.

Liquete, V., 2012. Can one speak of an "information transliteracy"? International Conference "Media and Information Literacy (MIL) for Knowledge Societies". Russian Federation, Moscow.

Liu, A., s.a. Transliteracies project: research in the technological, social, and cultural practices of online reading. University of California Santa Barbara. Available from: http://transliteracies.english.ucsb.edu/category/researchproject/rose (accessed 24.05.16.).

Lloyd, A., 2010. Information Literacy Landscapes: Information Literacy in Education, Workplace and Everyday Contexts. Chandos, Oxford.

Lupton, M., 2008. Information Literacy and Learning. Auslib Press, Adelaide.

Mackey, T.P., Jacobson, T.E., 2014. Metaliteracy: Reinventing Information Literacy to Empower Learners. Nael-Schuman, Chicago.

Megwalu, A., 2014. Transliteracy: a holistic and purposeful learning. Ref. Libr. 55, 381–384.

Megwalu, A., 2015. Encouraging transliteracy through reference instructions. Ref. Libr. 56, 157–160.

Miller, C., 2012. "Digital fluency": towards young people's critical use of the internet. J. Inf. Liter. 6, 35–54.

Oxford University Press. Oxford Dictionary of Literary Terms. 4th ed. S.l.: Oxford University Press.

Saracevic, T., 2014. Information literacy in the United States: contemporary transformations and controversies. In: Kurbanoglu, S., Spiranec, S., Grassian, E., Mizrachi, D., Catts, R. (Eds.), Information Literacy: Lifelong Learning and Digital Citizenship in the 21st Century; Second European Conference, ECIL 2014. Springer, Dubrovnik, Croatia.

SCONUL, 2011. The SCONUL seven pillars of information literacy: core model for higer education. Available from: http://www.sconul.ac.uk/sites/default/files/documents/coremodel.pdf (accessed 02.07.16.).

Smith, J.K., Given, L.M., Julien, H., Ouellette, D., Delong, K., 2013. Information literacy proficiency: assessing the gap in high school students' readiness for undegraduate academic work. Libr. Inf. Sci. Res. 35, 88–96.

Stordy, P., 2015. Taxonomy of literacies. J. Document. 71, 456–476.

Sukovic, S., 2014. iTell: transliteracy and digital storytelling. Austral. Acad. Res. Libr. 45, 205–229.

Thomas, S., 2013. Making a space: transliteracy and creativity. Digital Creat. 24, 182–190.

Thomas, S., Joseph, C., Laccetti, J., Mason, B., Mills, S., Perril, S., et al., 2007. Transliteracy: crossing divides. First Monday 12.

Transliteracy Research Group Archive 2006–2013, 2013. Available from: https://transliteracyresearch.wordpress.com/ (accessed 24.05.16.).

Tyner, K., 1998. Literacy in a Digital World: Teaching and Learning in Age of Information. Lawrence Erlbaum, London.

UNESCO, 2013. Media and Information Literacy: Policy and Strategy Guidelines. United Nations Educational, Scientific and Cultural Organization, Paris.

UNESCO, 2014. Records of the General Conference, 37th Session, Paris, 5–20 November 2013. The United Nations Educational, Scientific and Cultural Organization, Paris.

White, G.K., 2013. Digital fluency: skills necessary for learning in the digital age. ACER eSearch. Australian Council for Educational Research, Melbourne.

Study of transliteracy: approach

2

Transliteracy intuitively makes sense to many people, but what exactly does it mean? Answers to this deceptively simple question will be considered on the basis of many years of data-gathering in secondary and tertiary educational environments. In this chapter, research methodology and methods will be considered in some detail. Studies presented in this chapter were conducted in the period between 2004 and 2015 and they include several distinct projects with a common theme of learning and knowledge creation in interaction with digital technology. Although some of the projects were not initially developed with transliteracy in mind, they finally contributed to an understanding of this multilayered concept. But, before I present the studies, I would like to give the reader some sense of an idea development.

In the mid-1990s, I saw electronic literary and historical texts online for the first time and became fascinated by the possibilities they offered. The persistent question of how interactions with these texts could influence the ways we learn and think had led to my doctoral research. *Roles of Electronic Texts in Research Projects in the Humanities* is the title of my doctoral thesis, on which I worked between 2004 and 2007. Some intriguing parts of the findings related to the disappearance of clear delineation between different sources, genres, technologies, and research activities. Distinctions between academic and creative work, and rational and emotional insights, appeared increasingly blurry.

Soon afterwards I started working in a position in which I helped researchers to integrate technology in their research. At the time, Peter Read, a history professor at the University of Sydney, was starting his research project, *A History of Aboriginal Sydney*. Our discussions about the potential of online delivery to achieve one of his main goals, opening historical records to the community, led to the development of the project website. I developed the system architecture and web design for the site and remained involved in the project to some extent until its official conclusion at the beginning of 2015. During the project, digital delivery had become the main project focus and this, in turn, brought its own challenges and opportunities. The research team thrived on their enthusiasm for discovering traces of history in people's memories and the environment, and on a sense of purpose in returning historical records digitally to the Indigenous community. While responses by Indigenous, academic and professional communities were exceptionally positive, there were also questions about the nature of academic work. At the end of the project, I recorded interviews with some key team members about their experience of working on the project, aiming to deepen the understanding of a historical construction, achieved to a large extent by the use of digital technology.

Academics with whom I conducted interviews in the two studies, one into the roles of electronic texts and the other with members of the project team *A History of Aboriginal Sydney*, occasionally referred to the younger generations as those who

Transliteracy in Complex Information Environments. DOI: http://dx.doi.org/10.1016/B978-0-08-100875-1.00002-9

were more likely to feel at home with digital technologies and changing academic practices. Although research has shown that the notion of "digital natives" is not supported by the evidence (Miller, 2012; Cooper et al., 2013; Hinrichsen and Coombs, 2013; Smith et al., 2013; boyd, 2014; Lehmans and Cordier, 2014), I wondered if it was easier for younger generations to cross the lines between technologies and genres. If younger people do not have better information and digital skills than older people who grew up with analog technologies, perhaps they are more fluid and intuitive in their practices. An opportunity to investigate these questions presented itself when I started working as the head librarian at St. Vincent's College, an independent high school for girls in Sydney. In 2012, I initiated a digital storytelling project, iTell, as an action research project. Investigation of transliteracy was one of the main aims of the project. As iTell developed, transliteracy emerged as a very promising concept for education, and investigations branched out from digital storytelling into more mainstream classroom settings. By 2015, it became apparent that my other studies involving academics as participants could contribute valuable research data if considered from a transliteracy perspective. All the projects were explorations of how learning and knowledge construction develop, so the next step was to ask the same research questions of all the data that had been gathered over a decade.

The following sections provide some details of how the investigative process unfolded. The research approach and methodology are considered in some detail and the findings form a rich picture of transliteracy as a complex phenomenon.

2.1 Methodological approach

The study of transliteracy used predominantly qualitative methodology, which is suitable for research, given its exploratory nature. It is based on hermeneutics as a philosophy and a methodological approach. Philosophical understanding in this study is derived mainly from the work *Truth and Method* by a German philosopher, Hans-Georg Gadamer (2004). The philosophy of hermeneutics provides an interpretive framework for this methodological approach. Hermeneutical philosophy is closely aligned with phenomenology and their connection is apparent in hermeneutic phenomenology. As described by Sharkey (2001), hermeneutic phenomenology is used to understand subjective experiences and then move beyond them to understand underlying structures in these experiences. Hermeneutics provided a philosophical and methodological framework to uncover a range of perspectives leading to an understanding of transliteracy. The overall transliteracy study is an outcome of my prolonged presence in the field and work in professional and academic contexts.

An action research approach was used for research projects conducted in the high school setting because it suited the nature of practice-based research and is a well-established methodological approach in education (Holly et al., 2009). Action research cycles of planning, acting, observing, and reflecting are well aligned with the notion of the hermeneutic circle in which any understanding develops.

Mainly qualitative data-gathering methods were used in the study overall, in combination with some quantitative methods (e.g., surveys, counts of references to e-texts in participants' published or submitted works). Quantitative results were always considered in relation to other data and participants' interpretations.

A number of qualitative approaches are based on the integration of data collection and analysis. In the research projects as part of the transliteracy study, data were regularly analyzed and the results used to inform the next stages of data-gathering. Cycles of deductive and inductive reasoning unfolded as described by Strauss and Corbin (1998, pp. 136−137):

> Although statements of relationship or hypotheses do evolve from data [we go from the specific case to the general], whenever we conceptualize data or develop hypotheses, we are interpreting to some degree. To us, an interpretation is a form of deduction. We are deducing what is going on based on data but also based on our reading of that data along with our assumptions about the nature of life, the literature that we carry in our heads, and the discussions that we have with colleagues.

Data were gathered and analyzed with a multiplicity of perspectives and meanings in mind. Data were triangulated and findings probed as much as possible, with constant monitoring of variations in data and signs of contradictory evidence. Informal feedback from teachers and library staff in the high school context, as well as any significant observations from them, were documented in my research notes and included in the data mix.

2.1.1 Research questions

At the beginning of this chapter there was a reference to the development of ideas that connected initially separate research projects. At the center of all investigations was learning and knowledge production as it developed through the execution of substantial and information-rich tasks. High school students and academics worked on projects of different complexity, but all their work required some construction of meaning, investigation, and interaction with a range of sources and tools. All research data were collated and investigated from the perspective of the following research questions:

- What constitutes transliteracy?
- How do participants experience transliteracy?
- How does transliteracy contribute to participants' learning and knowledge production?
- What are some of the aids and challenges to transliteracy?

2.2 Data-gathering

All data in the study were gathered in high school and university settings. Individual projects, data-gathering methods, and characteristics of participants will be described for the two settings, with a cumulative summary of methods and participants given at the end. Unless stated differently, I developed and conducted all the projects.

2.2.1 High school setting

St. Vincent's College, an independent high school for girls in Sydney (Australia), has provided a fertile ground for data-gathering about transliteracy since 2012. Participants in transliteracy projects were girls in Years 7−10 (12−16 years of age), although observations were made about the development of earlier project participants as they progressed to senior years (Years 11 and 12). Students who participated in the projects were of mixed interests, backgrounds, and academic abilities. The socioeconomic backgrounds of participants in the transliteracy projects reflected the composition of the college student body. The projects included students from Sydney and boarders from small country towns. The majority were from middle-class families, but some were from a low socioeconomic background. After the first round of transliteracy-oriented projects, it became apparent that transliteracy programs may be particularly suitable for disengaged learners, so transliteracy projects and activities included a number of students who were often disengaged from learning in a regular classroom. In 2015, transliteracy investigations included work with regular classes to explore opportunities for working within the curriculum and investigate any bias involved in participants' self-selection.

Data were gathered with the intention of uncovering as many perspectives as possible. Particular attention was given to understanding student experience in the transliteracy projects. Surveys were given to students at the beginning of some projects to understand some general patterns in their learning. Surveys at the end of the projects provided initial data for further discussion in interviews and focus groups. Surveys also served as a suitable method of gathering individual data when it was not practical to organize further conversations with all students involved in a class-based learning experience. Final surveys also provided opportunities for students to express opinions anonymously. Semi-structured interviews were valuable for gathering in-depth data about individual experiences, while focus groups provided opportunities for considering a range of opinions and perceptions. Other forms of data-gathering, including interviews with and feedback from teachers, work samples, and school reports, provided a professional teacher perspective on student learning. Observation notes from library staff, in addition to those I made as a researcher, along with relevant feedback also from library staff, provided a variety of insights. A summary of data-gathering in the high school setting is provided in Table 2.1. In addition to the details provided below, further information about the projects and samples of student work are available from the college website (St. Vincent's College, 2015).

2.2.1.1 Digital storytelling project iTell

Digital storytelling is a term that loosely defines uses of well-known technologies to tell short, usually personal, stories. Text, pictures, and sound are combined to

Table 2.1 High school setting: data-gathering methods and participants

Project	#Student participants	Surveys #Student responses	Interviews	#Focus groups #Participants	Other forms of data-gathering
iTell	34	Initial #29 Final #16	9 (students)	1 (7 students)	Observation "One-minute paper"[a] Work samples Feedback from teachers and library staff School reports
Level Up	10	Initial and Final (all-10)	–	–	Observation Work samples Parent feedback
Languages Transliteracy Project	19	Final #13	1 (teacher)	1 (whole class-#19)	Observation Work samples Class discussion with Principal Feedback from the teacher and library staff
Enrichment Transliteracy Project	20	Final #16	–	2 (#7 and #4)	Observation Work samples Feedback from the teacher
Total	**83**	**84**	**10 (11 participants)**	**4 (37 participants)**	
Curriculum mapping pilots	Heads of Departments				Used to inform project development

[a]"One-minute paper"—Students were asked at the beginning of the workshop to briefly answer two questions on post-it notes expressing their hopes and "hope-nots" for the workshop.

present short presentations of a few minutes. Digital stories can be fictional or factual, but they should have a narrative.

Transliteracy investigations at the College were launched in 2012 with the initiation of iTell, which combined digital storytelling workshops with research. iTell was developed with the intention of developing student interest in reading and writing, and investigating boundaries between these activities. Students were invited to choose a book or an oral story they liked and use it as a basis for their digital story. They were encouraged to explore different perspectives, characters, and story lines, and take them in a new direction.

The workshops were normally conducted over a period of three or four days, usually starting with an afternoon session, followed by two whole consecutive days, with an additional session or two for students to finish the work. All workshops, with the exception of two days in one workshop, were delivered by the library staff, who also provided feedback for data-gathering. Software packages used in the workshops were those installed on school computers (e.g., Windows Moviemaker, image editor) or available for free download (e.g., Audacity).

Data were formally gathered in 2012 with some further targeted data-gathering in 2013. A combination of different forms of data-gathering aimed to uncover issues of student learning from various perspectives. Since then, iTell has become a regular annual event at the library and it has provided opportunities to monitor any changes in the way students work. Details about the organization of iTell and research findings, including many stories developed in the workshops, are available in Sukovic (2014) and on the college website.

2.2.1.2 Level Up

This project was developed and delivered in 2013 by a librarian, Alycia Bailey, aiming to teach students elements of game coding by using the software Kodu. Issues of transliteracy were explored by applying the research methodology developed for iTell, this time in relation to gaming. The thinking behind this approach was that the project would yield comparable data to enhance the existing data set. Level Up was offered in six weekly after-school sessions, each 1.5 hours long, to students who were members of the College Gaming Club.

2.2.1.3 Languages transliteracy project

In 2015, regular classrooms were included in explorations of transliteracy. During Term 3, transliteracy was explicitly included in teaching of the topic School Life in the Year 10 French class. In previous years, students had finalized the unit by presenting letters of recommendations for school improvement to the Principal. Letters were written in French, usually in a light-hearted manner. Students were assessed by oral examinations conducted in the form of in-class conversations with the teacher.

Julia Hegarty, language teacher and the acting Head of Languages, was interested in looking at different ways of delivering this unit and including transliteracy components in the existing program. We worked on adjusting the program to include explicit elements of transliteracy, aiming to gain some insights into transliteracy in the regular classroom setting to observe and analyze any effects of the changes. Edmodo, an online educational software platform working in the same way as Facebook, was used for class communication. Students prepared posters and letters to present their understanding of school life in France and Australia. They were asked to use Aurasma, an augmented reality software application, to attach videos and digital images to their posters. The Languages Department had been using videos in classes, so students were asked this time to prepare and record conversations about school life in pairs. These videos were used instead of oral examinations. They were watched by the whole class and students provided feedback to each other in addition to the teacher's comments and assessment. Students also presented their work to the Principal and discussed their learning experiences with her.

2.2.1.4   Enrichment project

Another project with a transliteracy component was initiated in Term 3, 2015 with two Year 9 Enrichment classes. Gifted and talented students were taken out from regular lessons once a fortnight. Enrichment coordinator, Cheryl McArthur, planned to start the topic *Truth and Reality* in Term 3 and was interested in shaping the topic to include transliteracy.

The unit was developed in the framework of inquiry-based learning. Students investigated a particular aspect of the topic throughout Semester 2. The two classes spent one or two whole days in the library to investigate the topic and had a range of electronic and physical resources available to them to guide their investigations. Transliteracy was explicitly included in whole-day sessions in the library and in presentation of student work. Students were given a variety of options for presentation at the beginning of the unit, ranging from journal articles to dance and drama performances, in addition to opportunities to use a range of technologies. They presented their work at the Enrichment Expo for parents, teachers, and other students as an audience. Their final presentations represented a variety of topics within the broad umbrella of *Truth and Reality* and a range of presentation options.

2.2.1.5   Curriculum mapping

There were two trials of curriculum mapping, which informed the development of the transliteracy initiative at the College. In the first pilot, a small working party developed a curriculum map of transferable skills for all subjects in Year 7, Semester 1. The group wrote a report with recommendations for the continuation of curriculum mapping. The next iteration was small-scale data-gathering for a curriculum map of transliteracy skills with a view to developing a cross-curricular transliteracy framework, starting with Year 7. Curriculum mapping is discussed in some detail in Chapter 4, *Transliteracy in Practice*.

Table **2.2** **University setting: data-gathering methods and participants**

Project	#Participants	#Interviews	Other forms of data-gathering
Roles of electronic texts	16	20	Audio-tapes with written comments (#2) Notes about other forms of data-gathering (i.e., examination of participants' work, data-gathering forms)
HoAS	3	3	Observations
Total	19	23	

Table **2.3** **University setting: participants' profile**

Gender	Field	Role/career stage
11 Female 8 Male	12 Historical studies 7 Literary studies	2 Early-career researchers 5 Mid-career researchers 11 Senior researchers (10 academic and research officer) 1 Support staff

2.2.2   University setting

Transliteracy in university contexts was seen through a lens of research in literary and historical studies. While all participants discussed their research projects, they also referred to their experiences with students related to the use of electronic resources and, in some cases, particular project outcomes related to teaching and education. A summary of data-gathering in the university setting is provided in Table 2.2 and a summary of participants' profiles in Table 2.3.

2.2.2.1   Roles of electronic texts in research projects in the humanities

As mentioned at the beginning of this chapter, the study under this title (above) was conducted for my doctoral thesis. The study explored interactions with e-texts and their role in research by looking into the development of participants' research projects. Sixteen historians and literary scholars from two major Australian cities and one participant from the United States discussed thirty research projects in interviews and provided data about their projects in other forms. Participants represented a variety of fields and disciplinary orientations and discussed projects on wide-ranging topics and time periods. Some of them conducted what is normally considered traditional humanities research, while others were deeply involved with the digital world. A study requirement, however, was to focus on research projects

Table 2.4 Data-gathering summary by sector

	High school	University	Total
Participants	83 students	19	**102**
Teachers, Library staff			
Interviews	10	23	**33**
Focus groups	4 (37 participants)	–	**4**
Survey responses	84	–	**94**
Audio tapes	–	2	**2**
Other forms of data-gathering	Yes	Yes	

aiming to produce traditional academic outputs. Details about sources of data for the study of transliteracy are presented in Table 2.2.

2.2.2.2   A History of Aboriginal Sydney

This five-year-long project was led by Professor Peter Read, a well-known scholar in the field of Australian Indigenous history. The project aimed to develop a reconstruction of Indigenous history in Sydney and make historical records available to Indigenous communities. The website "historyofaboriginal-sydney.edu.au" was developed with the idea of providing material for historical inquiries by the community, teaching and learning in high schools, and use by academic historians. A solution for the long-term archiving of research data was also part of the project. The project team included researchers, cinematographers, video editors, and web developers. At the end of the project, I conducted interviews with three key members of the team—Professor Peter Read, researcher Julie Janson, and a video editor, Chantal Jackson—about their experiences of working on the project.

An overview of data-gathering by high school and university sector is provided in Table 2.4. It provides an overview of the number of participants directly involved in the project, while the previous tables provided additional information about types of data-gathering.

2.2.3   Participants' privacy

Quotes from interviews and focus groups are used throughout this chapter. In order to protect participants' privacy, their names have been replaced with codes. The following abbreviations are used to assist the reader in identifying the relevant data-gathering settings and projects:

- HS—high school context
- U—university projects (other than HoAS)
- HoAS—History of Aboriginal Sydney.

These abbreviations are followed by more specific identifiers. Interviews with high school students are marked by a letter developed in a scheme to replace the initial of their first name. This technique protects student anonymity while avoiding confusion arising from names with the same initial letter. Focus group participants are not individually identified.

The research into the roles of electronic texts was initially developed in two stages. Recordings, transcriptions of interviews, and all other data were marked as Participant 1/1, 2/1, 1/2, and so on, with the first number identifying the participant and the second number indicating the first or the second stage of data-gathering.

Interviews conducted with members of the *History of Aboriginal Sydney* team are marked as HoAS, followed by the interviewee's name. HoAS team members did not think it was necessary to anonymize their interviews and preferred to be identified by their names.

Similarly, there was one interview with the French teacher, Julia Hegarty. All references to the "French teacher" in the quotes relate to the same person. One reference to the Drama teacher would be easily recognized by the school community. In both cases, teachers agreed that anonymity was not a concern.

In some instances, I highlighted relevant excerpts from research data or provided transcriptions of conversational exchanges. The letters "SS" in these excerpts indicate my initials.

2.3   Data analysis

A variety of data formats was used during the analysis. Surveys were delivered either as print surveys or online. Survey Monkey was used in both cases, either for survey delivery or data entry. All interviews were transcribed and focus group recordings were summarized and relevant passages transcribed.

The analysis phase of the study commenced during data-gathering, as is usual with the selected research approach and to aid my developing understanding. Data gathered from surveys were used to inform interviews. The outcomes of the interview analyses alerted me to issues to be addressed in subsequent interviews. Immersion in data through repeated listening to the recorded interviews and focus group discussions was part of the early stages of analysis. Even this early form of approaching the data promoted my understanding of common threads in the interviews and, in the long run, helped me in dealing with large amounts of data. Data-gathering and analysis were closely connected processes, not only because the analysis informed data-gathering but also because interview questions structured the data for analysis, which was particularly important in the early stages of analysis.

Data from interviews were used in audio and written forms simultaneously through a large part of the analytical process. I listened to recordings repeatedly to gain a sense of the whole interview and allow data to "speak for themselves" in context. After that, I proceeded to the initial coding of transcripts. Once I had developed an initial coding scheme, I started using the NVivo software and coded the written transcripts and summaries, often while listening to the tapes. Working with data in a variety of forms aided the process of answering questions suggested by Strauss and Corbin (1998): "What is going on here?" and "What makes this document the same as or different from the previous ones?"

Understanding developed by considering part and whole in the hermeneutic circle, which Schwandt described as a method:

> *The method involves playing the strange and unfamiliar parts of an action, text, or utterance off against the integrity of the action, narrative, or utterance as a whole until the meaning of the strange passages and the meaning of the whole are worked out or accounted for. [Thus, for example, to understand the meaning of the first few lines of a poem, I must have a grasp of the overall meaning of the poem and vice versa].*
>
> *Schwandt, 2001, p. 114*

A few layers of coding developed at different levels of abstraction in the process of comparing parts and the whole, and checking interpretations against data. Grounded theory techniques were used for coding. Open and axial coding were used in earlier stages of analysis and, later, selective coding. Open coding involved detailed line-by-line analysis, coding the sentence or paragraph and thinking about the whole document to identify the main concepts. "The *purpose of axial coding* is to begin the process of reassembling data that were fractured during open coding. In axial coding, categories are related to their subcategories to form more precise and complete explanations about phenomena" (Strauss and Corbin, 1998, p. 124). Selective coding involved the process of integration and refining of the analysis.

Analysis through comparisons was aided by the use of the flip-flop technique, which means asking the same question from the opposite direction (Strauss and Corbin, 1998), for example, asking what was helpful and what was not helpful in an interaction with online resources.

2.4 Credibility

All steps in the research process were carefully considered and documented to ensure the credibility of the study and the trustworthiness of research results. Triangulation provides the basis for phenomenological attempts to view phenomena from different perspectives, and triangulation of data sources and methods was used in this study. Triangulation of data sources was overviewed earlier in this chapter. Triangulation of methods was ensured by different data-gathering methods and analytical techniques, such as grounded theory techniques, the hermeneutic approach, and the quantitative analysis of survey data.

Prolonged engagement with the field of inquiry, avoiding the danger of "going native," and building trust with participants are some ways of ensuring credibility (Lincoln and Guba, 1985). Prolonged engagement with the field of inquiry was provided by my research and professional work in a university library prior to the commencement of the study of roles of electronic texts; data-gathering in this study over a period of almost two years; monitoring of related issues through a period of doing applied research, especially on the project *A History of Aboriginal Sydney*; and prolonged involvement with the transliteracy initiative in the school setting. Persistent data-gathering about participants' scholarly projects was ensured by using every opportunity to follow relevant developments in the projects under study, so I examined all relevant materials that were available, and attended seminars and workshops related to participants' work when opportunities arose. In the school context, I had opportunities to monitor student development over a period of several years. Persistent and prolonged engagement maximized opportunities to deepen my understanding of transliteracy. The danger of "going native" was avoided by the fact that I did not belong to participants' scholarly communities and, as a staff member, I was not part of student social groups. In the case of the project *A History of Aboriginal Sydney*, I was a member of the research team, but not part of the community of historians.

Documentation of the research process also contributes to credibility. Referential adequacy (Lincoln and Guba, 1985) and descriptive validity which concerns the factual accuracy of researchers' accounts (Maxwell, 2002) were ensured by taping and transcribing interviews and participants' comments as well as keeping samples of student work. Participants' published works also provided a reference point. Lincoln and Guba (1985) recommend that the researcher writes a reflexive journal about the research process and method to provide data about the research instruments that are used. Procedural and reflective memos were written during the individual research projects. Procedural memos were used to keep a record of the research process. Reflective memos were used to support the development of ideas by writing about them. The reading of memos aided the establishment of connections between ideas and ensured that various aspects of developing understanding were not lost in the large amount of data. In the school context, observational notes by librarians on the team enriched research documentation. Below are a couple of excerpts illustrating the notes taken during the study. The first excerpt is from my notes in the project *Roles of Electronic Texts in Research Projects in the Humanities* about theoretical sampling. The second excerpt is from the notes of a librarian who wrote up her observations about a group of students in iTell workshops.

> *Listening to all tapes several times made me aware that all participants have used etexts in addition to other sources. I would need to broaden the range and include one or two people who research electronic literature. I've checked biographical details of people in 3 institutions where I interviewed in Sydney and I don't think there is anyone who mainly does this sort of research...*
> *<Academic> from UNSW ... said that she hadn't used etexts much and recommended her predecessor who works in Canberra. I checked her details and she appears to be the right person... If I don't find anyone here, I'll have to travel to Canberra providing that this person wants to talk to me.*
> *[SS on theoretical sampling in the project* Roles of e-texts*]*

- *They are very technology savvy.*
- *When they were stuck on something to do with technology, they were happy to ask for help.*
- *When they were stuck on something to do with writing or story creation, they didn't ask for help. They would tune out instead—do something else, do nothing, etc.*
- *The girls seemed happy to talk about themselves or to present a personal story...*
- *Liked <Student's> story. Creative idea. A great sense of fun was demonstrated through her images.*
- *Thought <names of two students> stories were the most well spoken and thought through.*
- *Thought <Student> was quite into the whole program. She had a real go at all aspects—even the writing stages.*
  [Librarian's observations about iTell workshops]

Maxwell's approach to validity "refers primarily to accounts, not to data or methods" (Maxwell, 2002, p. 42). According to Maxwell, understanding is more fundamental than validity in qualitative research, but our experience cannot be validated independently of the observer. Observations by different people, especially in the high school setting, enhanced the validity of the findings. Interpretive validity relates to the interpretation of participants' perspectives. "Interpretive accounts are grounded in the language of the people studied and rely as much as possible on their own words and concepts" (p. 49). Interpretations of other people's accounts go beyond words to examine aspects that may be invisible or concealed by the people who are giving the accounts. Triangulation and techniques of data analysis in this study were used in a way that strengthened interpretive validity. The presentation of findings includes numerous accounts in participants' own words to provide evidence of interpretation.

In predominantly qualitative research projects, such as those which constitute the transliteracy study, external validity cannot be specified and the researcher "can provide only the thick description necessary to enable someone interested in making a transfer to reach a conclusion about whether transfer can be contemplated as a possibility" (Lincoln and Guba, 1985, p. 316). A detailed account of the research process and findings provides material for anyone who wants to consider the possibility of transfer.

2.5 Limitations, significance, and benefits

A limitation of the study is that it does not have statistical significance and cannot be generalized. The settings in which the study was conducted are similar to many others across the world, but they do not represent many contexts in which transliteracy could be observed elsewhere. Transliteracy, however, is always contextual and only a thorough understanding of different contexts can provide deep insights. Thick description in this study provides a touchstone for research-based understanding of similar groups and comparisons with different groups of people. Methodology described in this chapter could be used to investigate similarities and differences in other settings.

The significance of the study is that it is based on prolonged and thorough data-gathering and analysis, providing a wealth of data for an understanding of transliteracy. It grounds transliteracy as an abstract concept in the reality of learning and knowledge work. The study also contributes to our understanding of the impact of technologies on knowledge work. Although developments in the way we use technologies in our daily lives and work will continue, studies like this provide important reference points for the observation and understanding of significant societal changes.

The study is an example of transliteracy in its own right. It considers the work of high school students and academics in a continuum of knowledge work rather than separate categories. It also integrates theoretical and professional insights arising from the projects in university and library contexts, and contributes to bridging the gap between academia and the library and information profession.

Study results are applicable in the library and information field, education, and communication. Findings can be also used to inform professional development and learning in organizations.

2.6 Summary

This chapter provides details of a study, looking into transliteracy, on which this book is based. The study was guided by the following research questions:

- What constitutes transliteracy?
- How do participants experience transliteracy?
- How does transliteracy contribute to participants' learning and knowledge production?
- What are some of the aids and challenges to transliteracy?

The study was based on hermeneutics as a philosophy and methodological approach. It was conducted as a predominantly qualitative study using a variety of data-gathering methods over a long period of time. Data were gathered in high school and university settings. Action research was used in the high school setting. Data were analyzed by applying grounded theory techniques. Software applications NVivo and SurveyMonkey were used for analysis.

Methodology described in this book could be used for comparisons in other data-gathering settings, but the study does not have statistical significance. The significance of the study is that it is based on prolonged and thorough data-gathering and analysis, providing a wealth of data for an understanding of transliteracy. It grounds transliteracy as an abstract concept in the reality of learning and knowledge work. The study also contributes to our understanding of the impact of technologies on knowledge work.

References

boyd, D., 2014. It's Complicated: the Social Lives of Networked Teens. Yale University Press, New Haven.

Cooper, N., Lockyer, L., Brown, I., 2013. Developing multiliteracies in a technology-mediated environment. Educ. Media Int. 50, 93–107.

Gadamer, H.-G., 2004. Truth and Method. Continuum, New York.

Hinrichsen, J., Coombs, A., 2013. The five resources of critical digital literacy: a framework for curriculum integration. Res. Learn. Technol.21.

Holly, M.L., Arhar, J.M., Kasten, W.C., 2009. Action Research for Teachers: Traveling the Yellow Brick Road. Pearson, Boston.

Lehmans, A., Cordier, A., 2014. Transliteracy and knowledge formats. In: Kurbanoglu, S., Spiranec, S., Grassian, E., Mizrachi, D., Catts, R. (Eds.), Information Literacy: Lifelong Learning and Digital Citizenship in the 21st Century; Second European Conference, ECIL 2014. Springer, Dubrovnik, Croatia.

Lincoln, Y.S., Guba, E.G., 1985. Naturalistic inquiry. Sage Publications, Beverly Hills, CA.

Maxwell, J.A., 2002. Understanding and validity in qualitative research. In: Huberman, M.A., Miles, M.B. (Eds.), The Qualitative Research's Companion.

Miller, C., 2012. "Digital fluency": towards young people's critical use of the internet. J Inf Lit. 6, 35–54.

Schwandt, T.A., 2001. Dictionary of Qualitative Inquiry. Sage Publications, Thousand Oaks.

Sharkey, P., 2001. Hermeneutic phenomenology. In: Barnacle, R. (Ed.), Phenomenology. RMIT University Press, Melbourne.

Smith, J.K., Given, L.M., Julien, H., Ouellette, D., Delong, K., 2013. Information literacy proficiency: assessing the gap in high school students' readiness for undergraduate academic work. Libr Inf Sci Res. 35, 88–96.

St.Vincent's College, L.R.C., 2015. Transliteracy. St. Vincent's College, Potts Point, Sydney. Available from: http://www.stvincents.nsw.edu.au/learning/learning-resource-centre/teaching-and-learning/practice-based-research/transliteracy/ (accessed 27.12.15).

Strauss, A., Corbin, J., 1998. Basics of Qualitative Research: Techniques and Procedures for Developing Grounded Theory. Sage Publications, Thousand Oaks.

Sukovic, S., 2014. iTell: Transliteracy and Digital Storytelling. Austral. Acad. Res. Libr. 45, 205–229.

Exploring transliteracy

3

Transliteracy is an ability to use diverse analog and digital technologies, techniques, modes, and protocols to search for and work with a variety of resources; to collaborate and participate in social networks; and to communicate meanings and new knowledge by using different tones, genres, modalities, and media. Transliteracy consists of skills, knowledge, thinking, and acting, which enable fluid "movement across" in a way that is defined by situational, social, cultural, and technological contexts.

This definition of transliteracy, introduced in Chapter 1, *Introduction*, arose from the research data. In this chapter, research findings will be presented to ground the elusive concept of transliteracy in the reality of knowledge work. The conceptual model of transliteracy will be presented and then used to frame explorations of what constitutes transliteracy. Participants' experiences of transliteracy, and what it contributes to their learning and knowledge production, will be discussed in the second part of this chapter.

3.1 The conceptual model

The proposed model of transliteracy aims to bridge the gap between the fluidity and broad meaning of the concept, and its application in practice. The conceptual model is developed with the idea that transliteracy happens as part of lifelong learning and in a variety of formal and informal contexts. Transliteracy comes to the fore in information- and technology-rich environments, so it is based on information and ICT (information and communications technology) capabilities. It also encompasses creativity, critical thinking, and communication and collaboration. These are the main skill and knowledge components of transliteracy. These defining components are not situated wholly in the transliteracy framework, as they can be observed regardless of transliteracy. Literacy and numeracy underpin transliteracy in the same way as they enable any learning (Fig. 3.1).

The words "capability," "literacy," "skill," "capacity," carry complex connotations so it is worth focusing on the word choices for a moment. In the phrases "information capability" and "ICT capability," the word "capability" has been chosen because of its broad meaning and emphasis on "ability." "Information skills" and "information literacy" are very common phrases in the library field, but they are rarely used by academics and university students in relation to their own knowledge and skills. They are not commonly used in relation to the professional development or work-related skills and capacities either. Since transliteracy is by its nature cross-disciplinary, it makes sense to use the language that is amenable for

Transliteracy in Complex Information Environments. DOI: http://dx.doi.org/10.1016/B978-0-08-100875-1.00003-0

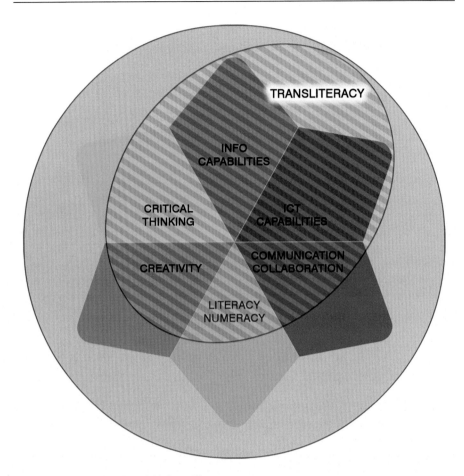

Figure 3.1 Conceptual model of transliteracy.

other disciplines and in nonlibrary contexts. The word "capability" emerged through an alignment with education and the current prominence of the term in Australian educational terminology. In the Australian Curriculum, general capabilities refer to seven components, including ICT capability, and creative and critical thinking: "General capabilities ... encompass knowledge, skills, behaviors and dispositions that, together with curriculum content in each learning area and the cross-curriculum priorities, will assist students to live and work successfully in the twenty-first century" (ACARA, 2013, para 1).

The word "capability" is also commonly used by universities to denote graduate outcomes, and the phrase "professional capabilities" denotes standards and frameworks for professional development in many fields. The word "capability" is likely to be readily recognized and accepted outside the library and information world. At the same time, library and information professionals can easily understand it in terms of "skills" and "literacy."

The term "ICT" also requires a closer look in the context of transliteracy. It normally refers to digital technologies. However, the book, radio, and television are also technologies designed to carry information and facilitate communication. The development of digital technologies required new terminology, but it is time to revisit the labels. The novelty of computers distinguished them from the rest, and so did their size and function. Large computers and TV sets imposed a sense that we were dealing with different technologies. At the same time, books and pens were so common and familiar that they were not perceived as a technology. They were also comparatively small and easy to use, so they did not demand special attention. Since then, digital devices are becoming increasingly integrated into the environment, smaller, and familiar. It is not obvious anymore how to distinguish between digital services and devices. Televised programs can be played on a range of devices, so the TV set loses its distinguished presence in our living rooms and lives. We used to know what we meant by "pen and paper," but with new digital technologies, the lines distinguishing the computer on one side, and pen and paper on another, are less obvious. Aren't they all writing and drawing devices anyway? At the same time, old familiarities fade and we need to remember that book indices and street directories in book form are alien technologies for many young people, while revamped vinyl records are now in the domain of music connoisseurs, many of them hipsters and millennials.

In the spirit of convergence, it is time to revisit the term "ICT." In order to understand and appreciate transliteracy, it is helpful to understand "ICT" as a label for analog and digital information and communication technologies, and their many combinations. Which ones we need to adopt and know should be a decision determined by the context and relevant evidence.

3.2   What constitutes transliteracy?

Researchers have always worked with all the materials they could access and used technologies available to them. What has changed? Is there anything qualitatively new in the way we work now? The snapshot below, written by a historian and study participant, Professor Peter Read, provides an insight into research as it was 30 years ago and now (Read, 2016). It opens considerations of transliteracy as a unique concept.

1986
My first day in the History Department of the Research School of Social Sciences, Australian National University. I am to begin a biography of Charles Perkins, first Indigenous Head of a Federal Government department. A senior historian tells me that computers are a waste of time. Only five years ago, at the Institute of Aboriginal Studies all of one's writing went on the very inadequate mainframe computer, so that one's typing on the screen was always at least a sentence or two behind. After lunch, when everyone came back to work, it was sometimes a whole hour behind.

A key element of the biography will be taped interviews, done on a state-of the-art Nagra reel to reel belonging to the National Library of Australia. At maximum reproduction, it uses a doubletrack reel in half an hour, which means that Charles, like all interviewees, tends to become fixated as it nears the end of each tape, and shapes the length of his answers accordingly. Each interview I'll summarize on 4 by 6 inch file cards to be stored alphabetically in a wooden box. The other research element in the biography will be Charles' private and Departmental material he will make available to me. For the rest of research, secondary texts won't be much use to me as very few contain any oral history.

2015

My project on the history of Aboriginal Sydney has turned into a website. As in 1986, oral evidence will be critical, but now I use video instead of audio, as cameras are cheap, easy to use and a much more useful means of mass communication. There are lots of Stolen Generation oral history stories online because they were collected as part of the Bringing Them Home package, and held in the National Library. You can hear them as well as read them, and use keywords to not only get to the tape transcript but inside the tape itself, so you hear the voice on the keyword you've searched for. But oral history online always represents last year's or last decade's concerns. If you want new stuff or the latest thinking, then get your camera and get out to do it yourself. The kind of archival record I used for Perkins is pretty well closed up, but luckily I've read much of it before the government sealed it up permanently. That's a real tragedy for the future knowledge of our nation's past: governments have learned that their archival records are potentially dynamite and close them to protect privacy. How convenient!

Many of my colleagues at Sydney University, I suspect, don't approve of the website, but my answer is that we historians have always tried to research, analyze and communicate. That's what websites do too, but to a mass audience instead of one or two thousand. In an academic article I have video clips to insert instead of verbatim quotes.

I also work in Pinochet-era Chilean history where oral elements are just as crucial if one wants to say anything new. But now almost everything I need is online. All the disappeareds are in one Archive (the Valech report) and all the torture victims are listed in the other government report. In getting the political slant of the various parties, however obscure, there is the instant information along with testimonies and all sorts of things which might have been first published, say, in the 1990s. This cannot replace talking to people who happen to have ephemeral documents in their possession still, but the amount of information which private political parties and interest groups put up is mind boggling.

In this study, transliteracy is considered as part of the information tasks and research projects. In asking what constitutes transliteracy, the question is less about information phases and tasks, and more about the qualities of behaviors and practices observed in the study. The creation of digital stories, interactive databases, and an augmented reality experience for the audience all fit into the final stages of the information and research processes. They are also outcomes of transliterate ways of exploring the content, which are based on well-established information practices. Transliteracy, however, comes to the fore in the process of remixing resources and protocols, and recombining established practices to open new information and knowledge spaces.

Key elements in defining transliteracy are related to diverse ways of working with the multiplicity of resources and working with others. The former is mainly situated in the information section of the transliteracy model, while the latter mainly relates to the collaboration and communication. Presentation of work is a form of communication, but strongly based on interaction with resources. Working with information resources and people is enhanced by ICT capabilities. Creativity and critical thinking remain constantly present in varying degrees.

3.2.1 Working with resources

There's a vast ocean of information out there and I can draw on that when I feel like it.

Participant 9/1.

A deluge of accessible resources as a major achievement of the digital age has become a trope in contemporary writing. Despite all the problems associated with a wealth of information and access privileges, a variety of resources is a cornerstone of transliterate behaviors and experiences. Resources for transliteracy are outlined in this section by considering the significance of multiplicity of resources with different qualities and provenance, information retrieval and the purpose of accessing multifarious sources. Discussions about the use of resources mainly relate to information capabilities in the transliteracy model (Fig. 3.2). It is important to bear in mind, however, that categories and placements are tentative and constantly shifting in transliteracy.

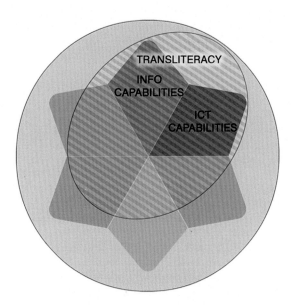

Figure 3.2 Working with resources.

3.2.1.1   Multiplicity of resources

A transliterate way of working often begins with the availability of resources in different formats. It is well established that academics in the humanities need a variety of resources from different time periods to conduct their research (Wiberley and Jones, 1989; Sze and Ngah, 1997; Palmer and Neumann, 2002; RULOIS, 2002; Houghton et al., 2003; Dalton and Charnigo, 2004; Palmer, 2005; Al-Shboul and Abrizah, 2014). Traditional academic resources are normally accessed in archives, libraries, personal collections and, sometimes, in oral history. Availability of alternative resources representing different voices, tones, and genres, in addition to traditional academic resources, can stimulate exploration and thinking. For example, a historian who researched perceptions of Captain Cook from the perspective of cultural studies used a wide range of information sources, including objects and websites. The researcher was interested in "Cook kitsch" and found links made on commercial sites quite useful. Another historian used images, maps, government records, and GPS (Global Positioning System) data, among other information sources, and found digitized collections particularly useful. Similarly, students in the Enrichment classes started explorations for their *Truth and Reality* project with experiments to investigate reliability of sensory information, eLibrary guides consisting of videos, databases, and catalog records, as well as a box full of books providing easy access to a range of scientific and philosophical ideas for further explorations.

In all these cases, multiplicity of resources provides not only more information, but also a wider variety and granularity of information that can be used for different purposes. Different modes of interaction with sources of information open pathways for multimodality at later stages of a project. I have observed this with high school students, when embedding multiplicity and multimodality at early stages of exploration implicitly scaffolds the next stages of research. In a different way, the creation of digital stories as practiced in iTell starts with watching examples of digital stories, and then a range of ideas raised during playful activities and conversations is employed to prepare the next stages of multimodal work. In research and creative contexts alike, a variety of information sources feeds understanding through transliteracy.

What often happens now as blogging kind of culture emerges more and more strongly, something like oral history often gets captured in blogging culture. So if one did a search on [Australian historical personality], one might find a few blog entries as well as … local historical society online postings about him. So there you've got a whole range of different registers of different genres of text all turning up in the electronic version. (U Participant 13/1)

    Because when you're dealing with something like popular culture, the things that become your primary sources are sometimes quite extraordinarily banal, seemingly banal things—like a box of toffees called Captain Cook Toffees, like tourist trips on replicas of the Endeavour. They actually operate as primary sources. But we also use the primary sources which are things like his original journals. We use

(Continued)

> **(cont'd)**
>
> *things like the Cook Society web pages to see how many people log on and what they say. We use, again—these things appear in both electronic and non-electronic texts, for example tourist guides, where you can go to see him and suggestions of itineraries, etc. And then, of course, all the accounts of Cook. (U Participant 7/1)*
> *So this offered, this particular project, because it involved the digitisation of* **ordinary people's photographs***, which didn't leave their possession, it gave us a massively democratised access to images. And the fact that they were ... searchable by caption, owner, date, location was a huge advance on the way that we could use our time for image research. So it textualised, if you like, it put language, searchable language onto images. Now, arising, the next thing that happened was that the Public Works Department digitised its entire collection and made that available through the State Library, with the same enormously easy mode of access. And, now, more recently, all of that's gone up on the web. So you can search that plus a whole— everything else is there. (U Participant 3/1, emphasis by SS)*

3.2.1.2   Information retrieval

A key aspect of accessing and using information is constant movement across a range of resources and practices. Information searching and selection taps into various skills and abilities as people manage an often frustrating process of finding relevant resources. Managing high recall and relevance is a challenge for academics and students alike. For a senior historian, there is no substitute for intuition once search techniques are exhausted.

Skills for handling diverse retrieval systems as well as understanding the potential future use(s) of information are often critical. A media historian explained how she used card catalogs, keyword searching across several databases, and visual display of audio files, in addition to archivists' assistance, to locate relevant documents. This researcher used photocopied documents in combination with a File Maker database and the referencing software, EndNote, to keep track of resources and recorded excerpts. She explained how her decisions about recording relevant information during searching were often based on her prediction of its future use.

> *I had to bring my background knowledge a bit to it because I have done digital editing before… If I hadn't have that background knowledge, I think it would've been a bit daunting, especially if I wasn't familiar with searching electronic text. Basically I had to use three different catalogues to find this material and that was to my own lateral thinking that I came with some of these things, and the help of the researchers there.*
> *U Participant 2/2 comments*

3.2.1.3   Purpose of multiplicity of resources

Information retrieval across different systems may be skilled, even impressive, work but the questions about its purpose remain. Why does it matter? Didn't researchers access all kinds of information and produce ground-breaking research before the advent of digital media and the Internet?

The importance of access to a range of electronic and analog sources is a matter of degree for different researchers. Support for new lines of investigation is the main reason for working across resources and technologies. An exploration of patterns of available, and gaps formed by absent, information is a critical part of research.

> ... *to be able to search everything that relates to a particular topic over some decades and across a number of newspapers is just fantastic.* **And it gives a whole added ability to make comparisons and to do better research**. *(U Participant 3/1, emphasis by SS)*
>
> *Through the project I became more and more reliant, really, on search engines. Not for the final conclusive material necessarily, but to help me see patterns, to search on a particular set of search words or look for a particular piece of evidence or try to trace a character. And I tried to trace that character from several different directions or using several different search methods, you could often start to build up a profile of that because you get the information in a patterned way. So using search engines was extremely useful. (U Participant 13/1)*
>
> *You can type that into JSTOR and ... you can get a few things, and you can trace absences as well as presence, if you like, the presence of a particular research topic. (U Participant 14/1)*

Researchers who use information for academic and creative writing rely on the Internet, films, daily papers, academic databases, and anything that could be relevant to work across knowledge domains: "It [electronic text] offers alternate points of view, it allows me to add gravitas or all those kinds of things I associate with research, academic research. But with fiction, I suppose it allows me to feed an imaginative process" (U Participant 1/2).

Senior researchers with many years of experience compared their past research with what they are able to do with digital information and found significant qualitative differences. The way Participant 6/1 explained this is that digital information allows "pursuing the sort of question that just'd be so uneconomic to ask, going in fishing, pot luck to see what turns up." He gave an example of one of the first projects in which he used digital methods. He bought time on a mainframe computer and entered a large sample of 17th century texts, spending a great deal of time and effort on work that could be easily done on a desktop computer a few years later:

> *It was just enormously primitive. But even in those days, it allowed you to ask questions you wouldn't bother asking otherwise because it would take too long to find out and you wouldn't know whether the answer was significant. ... I have found that electronic text does allow that sort of—oh, what would happen if I asked this question or what would happen if...*
>
> U Participant 6/1

In a similar vein, a historian explained how the practicalities of doing research influence research decisions: "Now, we couldn't have even begun to do those searches with the limited amount of time and resources, if we were doing it in hard copy. And we wouldn't actually have imagined making those sorts of links because it wouldn't be simple to do so we wouldn't have even bothered" (U Participant 3/1). A senior researcher prepared an edition of old Nordic letters and found electronic dictionaries very helpful. When asked how she did that type of work in the past, she answered,

> *I don't know. I didn't. [laughs]. I didn't do this particular job before—I suppose you'd just have to go to encyclopedias and you'd have to go to expanded dictionaries, print dictionaries and what not. You probably could get the same information, but it would probably take you longer. And you wouldn't necessarily have quite the same level of up to date secondary information that came with it because when I did these dictionary searches, I not only . . . found out where the word 'rainfall' was, but also where it was located in a particular modern edition. And I couldn't necessarily got that from some old dictionary.*
>
> *U Participant 12/1*

The amount of information changes the way researchers work with significant implications for both the type of research that is done and the academic culture that supports it, which will be discussed in Chapter 5, *Transliterate Cultures*. A historian described the main difference between how research was done in the past and how it is now in the following way:

> *Great scholar from say the 13th century or the 14th century, like Roger Bacon, when he died he owned 37 books. And this was a huge library . . . And he'd saved all his money and he'd spent it all on these books and he probably had read every one of them several hundred times because there were so few of them. I own over 4,000 books and of course I don't read, I don't know them intimately in that sense. I think of them always as something to draw upon, a resource, and I think of what my computer can bring me in much the same way. **It's like there's a vast ocean of information out there and I can draw on that when I feel like it.***
>
> *U Participant 9/1, emphasis by SS*

3.2.1.4   Transliterate explorations

The previous consideration of the purpose of a variety of resources for transliteracy opens a largely uncharted territory of transliterate explorations. A range of materials, modes, and technologies often lead to transliterate practices in working with materials and establishing unexpected connections. Individual, rather than authorial or authoritative, interpretations come to the fore in these interactions. New approaches to overcoming obstacles also become possible.

A number of researchers discussed how they can do research that was impossible in working with analog materials only. In the case of HoAS, the decision was made to present historical research for community use. Video interviews captured oral testimonies as well as nonverbal clues while a digital timeline and map visualized historical information. The website later became an important resource for new historical projects. Peter Read described his research, which resulted in a book, and discussed how the website helped him to locate information. Visual details informed and ignited thinking:

> *...that would be possible anyway, but I wouldn't be able to put my finger nearly so quickly on what I know because I wouldn't be able to conceptualize the history of river as I was talking to people and put it in a visual form. You may think there isn't a big difference between putting it in a visual form and doing it anyway but, to me, there is. I know exactly what I need to do next. When I do the next chapter, the 1950s, I think instinctively "who I'll use for that, where are they living, what are the visuals I have in mind". In the 1950s, this [area] is the edge of Sydney. There was a big note "no road here".*
>
> HoAS, Peter Read

Interactions with digital information promote the idea of montage and collage. Multimodal interactions were compared with music as quick movements among pieces of information promote the juxtaposition of ideas.

> Participant 13/1 discussed his exploration of jazz movements in America in the 1950s, describing how he would read about Charlie Parker, then look for information about clubs or a jazz band, before returning to the main text:
>
> *And in a way, you're actually thinking and putting things together in a pattern that's very similar to the patterns of that particular culture. It's quick explorations jumping over to possible relationships elsewhere, jumping back to your main theme that you're playing variations on. On some websites as well, of course, you can get little sound files that help you understand, listen to the thing that is being described verbally as well. So just the way that you can investigate your way towards an understanding of a topic in some of these born digital texts strikes me as a very, very good and useful way of knowing... It's simply a different way of coming to know, not necessarily better, but different from reading one very, very good book on Charlie Parker. (U Participant 13/1)*
> *... you've got a couple of different documents open and you're cutting and pasting or you're toddling between two or three documents, and you're just feeling ideas come out of this idea, idea no 1 and idea no 2, when they pop up against each other often completely other idea, idea no 25 will, sort of, turn up out of that... That also can happen when you're zooming through the television as well and when you're skipping between all sorts of media, but it's easier to do that now, of course, with our digital formats, so that's the montage idea. (U Participant 6/2)*

Transliterate explorations promote individual interpretation instead of relying on the author's authority. Study participants from the HoAS team commented on how no one will watch hundreds of videos and explore every detail on the site. The site was designed for every user to create his or her own path. Not only did Peter Read find the website useful for his new project, as described above, but he believed that the information is always open for new constructions: "I always maintain that if you want to write a PhD on the history of Sydney, you can write a hell lot of it just looking at the website. And not to make the links that we do, you may, there are many of them, but for you as a historian to make the links, which there is always that point of call."

With the shift from the defined to open-ended meanings, transliteracy provides opportunities for exploring ideas from a new angle and using them creatively. In digital storytelling workshops, a number of students found that games were a useful way of starting to understand new perspectives in a story:

> *My favourite one was with the Goldilocks when we all had to be different pieces of furniture and we gave them a personality, where it's like you walk in, you think of a story and you only think of the, not even the animal characters, you only think of the human ones, so it was good to look at the inanimate objects. And think, "Oh okay... well... what does the pencil case feel like when Boo Radley is walking around the house?" It was a nice start. That one was one that I found most effective in a way. Cos I've always wanted to look at inanimate objects but never really... really looked at them.*
>
> *HS N.*

An academic described how a variety of information from public documents and conversations with witnesses of studied events was used creatively outside the intended meaning in information sources:

> *... battle sites and ... they were important, not from a military point of view but because of things like the fact the French called their ... hm... camps, they gave their camps women's names, so little things like that were actually imaginatively used. I had the children in the book calling their dolls after these camps. So it was useful not because it was military information but because it was something that could turn into what I wanted to do with it.*
>
> *U Participant 1/1*

Similarly, participants discussed how they used technology and different approaches to solve problems and resolve obstacles. Digitization of textual and audio documents in analog forms has been mentioned several times to describe different ways of managing information. Participant 10/1, for example, used a small tape recorder in situations where he could not take photocopies or photographs of hard-copy materials and recorded his reading of the content, which would be later transcribed. This academic had a large collection of documents in hard and electronic formats, organized to enable different access points aiding retrieval and exploration.

A high school student used a clever combination of her own pictures and newspaper images not only to create an individual expression, but also to overcome some limitations of readily available images. This student also recorded her story based on some notes to avoid writing, which she found difficult. The use of digitally manipulated images and audio-recordings enabled her to express nuanced ideas, which she could not convey in writing alone.

The use of technology and multimodal ways of working was particularly reward-ing for some people when it involved creativity and lateral thinking. A researcher who worked with audio files enthusiastically explained how she used her back-ground knowledge to access information in a multimodal manner:

So what's interesting about that... is really a different way of interacting with the text completely because usually, with audio, you may have some written text, which is coming up in front of you on the screen while you are listening to it from the tape or whatever. But in this, it is actually integrated into the file, so the way I can explain that is that you can search by keywords and so on actually in the file while it's there in front of you. But it also has a visual aspect, which you don't get in other media because the file actually comes up as a sound sample file so you can actually see the peaks and the trots as you're going along. It's actually a bit like being an editor because you can go backwards and forwards, highlight things, skip around, you just interact with the audio in a very different way. So I was looking at quite long files, maybe an hour or even up to an hour and a half, and I was able to go through and find particular points that I wanted, skip backwards and forwards very easily and transcribe them very quickly.

U Participant 2/2

Choosing the best technique to capture information may involve transliterate ways of both gathering and presenting data. In the following and other instances observed in the study, a line between the gathering and creating of information is often barely discernible:

We're using a combination of hard copy, draft maps, which we take to the interviews and we get people to draw on them the way they move around the parks...which parks they go to. And we are also planning to work with a handheld GIS recorder and actually doing some of these walks with people. So that will, we'll try and see which of those two methods allows us to most accurately plot both the pathways and the places.

U Participant 3/1

The planned outputs from this project included a combination of marked maps, excerpts from interviews, and academic publications. Data-gathering and communi-cation of results become closely connected.

3.2.2   Working with others

So that whole people-publication, actually "humanly connecting with them" thing works.

Participant 7/1

If there is one area where meanings of common phrases associated with knowledge work are noticeably shifting, it is in social aspects of transliteracy. The simple expres-sion "working with others" evokes ideas of a team, workshop, or a group of people

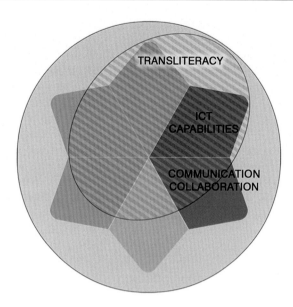

Figure 3.3 Working with others.

around a table. "Working with others" in a transliterate sense, however, may include anything between a team collaboration on the same project to responding to a request for information from a stranger we may receive as individuals, rather than in our official capacity, via the Internet. While the meaning of "working with others" in the first instance is clear, the latter requires a leap of imagination to envisage a culture of connectivity. "Working with others" is becoming a continuum in which reference points stretch from close collaboration to remote communication with strangers. Teamwork, cooperation, communication for assistance and communication with the audience are part of the continuum. In transliterate ways of working and communicating, the audience can become the source of information and collaborator in a broad sense.

Collaboration and cooperation will be considered in some detail in this section, and presentation of research results discussed as part of communication. As Fig. 3.3 illustrates, the focus will shift to the collaboration and communication, enabled by ICT capabilities.

3.2.2.1 Collaboration and cooperation

Collaboration and cooperation in situations when people know details of each other's work and interact easily are conducive to transliteracy. For some participants, close collaboration and a sense of connection were promoted through transliterate ways of working.

For students in iTell, a sense of connection and learning from peers was one of the key aspects of their experience. In the first round of workshops, most students worked individually on their story, except one large group, which created a collaborative story. Other students were very interested in the collaborative creative process they observed and expressed interest in working in this way. In subsequent rounds of iTell, increasing numbers of students decided to work in groups. In the last rounds of iTell, most students worked in groups. Similarly, students in the Enrichment project discussed the advantages of working in close proximity and learning from peers, and expressed a desire to have the option of working in pairs in the future.

Working on individual projects in close proximity with peers who knew about each other's work and had a sense of a common goal was described as a powerful aspect of learning. French students explained in the focus group how important it was to "go off each other," borrow ideas, and have a real conversation in French when they were recording their videos. A creative student who dealt with personal and social issues described how this way of working in iTell helped her to get to know people and feel less shy and more creative. Another student described the experience in iTell: "When we were all sitting there together and talking about things, it felt like we got a lot done and we all had the same common goal so we were talking about that and it was good" (HS M.). Student N. described the benefits of working together:

> *You feel a lot more comfortable in the atmosphere, like you've got the librarians that you can talk to for adult guidance or you can ask your peers, like I asked India and Tayla what I should do here and I got them to look at it and they asked if I could look at theirs. And it was basically every single person's movie was the whole by the end of it. And also working with more students meant more movies to look at. It was definitely better in that aspect where you can get a whole group of movies and say, 'this is what we've done' instead of just having one movie. I reckon that by having groups it was definitely more beneficial.*

A new media scholar described the importance of developing networks in establishing new ways of working. Similarly to students, he appreciated informal support and mentioned the example of a friend and colleague who had found some information he sought after an informal conversation.

Explorations of transliterate ways of working often include new forms of cooperation, which may change the meaning of authorship. A talented young writer who usually worked on her own found out that group experience in iTell made her interested in collaborative writing:

> *M.: Doing your own story is really fun but it would be good to have input from other people and to have, like, to do things with other people so you're not just by yourself the whole time...*
> *SS: But then your idea may get lost. Is that okay with you?*
> *M.: Yeah, I think that's alright sometimes because you have to compromise, but you come out with a different story at the end, something you might never have thought of by yourself.*

The HoAS website, for example, is inevitably a result of collaborative effort. Peter Read discussed in some detail the 19th century notion of the "great oeuvre" and the single authorial voice, as opposed to the collaborative work common in creating music. "Websites are most inevitably, and they should be, collective endeavors," he commented. With significant contributions from the team, the issue of inclusion goes beyond acknowledgment and becomes a matter of representing the variety of voices and emotions people bring into the project: "What's the best way to communicate the strong feelings of all of these who created this project, not to mention the people in it? How are we going to communicate those feelings in the digital website? I haven't thought about that before. Interesting" (HoAS, Peter Read).

New ways of collaborating, sometimes with changing levels of involvement, raise critical questions about the development of ideas and authorship. While purely individual authorship has arguably never existed, considering that complex influences and intertextual dialogs have always been part of any creation, new forms of working raise increasingly pressing questions about the inclusion of various forms of collaboration in systems of evaluation and acknowledgment.

3.2.2.2 Communication

Communication permeates transliterate ways of working. The ease of getting in touch with strangers and the existence of online social protocols, which make this sort of communication acceptable, influence how people go about finding information. Seeking information from strangers, who may become part of an information chain or future collaborators, is integral to research projects. Participant 7/1 summarized the process in the following way:

So when you found someone in particular who had written something you really like and then written it in the last two years and their email address was at the bottom, so you could actually also realise you could go and talk to them. And then if you like them, you could connect them in with your Cook network. So that whole people-publication, actually 'humanly connecting with them' thing works.

In a project which aims to provide historical information to the community, communication with the public becomes a part of connecting with the community, while information seeking and provision become part of the circle of social connection:

But one of the most exciting things that happened this week was people writing in to say, "I am [related] to people who are connected with Maramarra Creek in Hornsby River. I am one of the lost branches of the family, do you think you can help me to get in touch with the people?" We send it all around the family, other people who may be interested in replying and say, "See, would you like to reply?" And, of course, they did. But, also, "Could you send me a copy of the replies and what's going on?"

HoAS, Peter Read

Read reflected on his career as a historian and concluded that "if I contributed anything new to the historical writing, I've been good at integrating written source with the people." In his current and future work, knowing "what's going on," in combination with written sources, is a key aspect of his "presenting history in terms of living people." When asked if the website helped him to be in touch more with real people, he answered, "And communicate with them as well. Both those things."

The act of presenting one's work online has some impact on the creative process. When students record their French conversations to be viewed by the class and potentially be published online, or when they make a video experiment for their *Truth and Reality* project, to be presented to an audience, they think about the quality of their work and the performance aspects more carefully. The French teacher stressed the importance of working in this way, "that the kids become the author of something that is available to a bigger variety of people rather than just using the exercise book and me marking it and giving it back."

Various networks are formed in communication and they, in turn, start defining new ways of working. Participant 15/1 commented on how emerging lines of research in new media often start from English departments: "It's just that when you're one of the first ones to do it, you're not aware that that's what's happened until you start getting various kinds of feedback, [develop an] emerging network of contacts, you realize, 'oh, it's no longer English space, it's now something else.'" New ways of communicating online bring multiple voices into research and start changing its direction:

> *But you got to appreciate, it's not just communicating in a different way, as you are, but you also, you are not the sole voice any more. If you are, go and do something else. But others are working there and there are the voices of your collaborators, and to some extent the voices of the people who are involved, which you always incorporate in your work anyway. Really, I don't know where it's going to end, but I think it's a good direction to think about.*
>
> *HoAS, Peter Read*

3.2.2.3 Netchaining

Chaining, browsing, networking, and communication are combined seamlessly in information seeking. "Netchaining is about establishing and shaping information chains, which link sources and people" (Sukovic, 2008, p. 274). New patterns of information seeking and communication were revealed in the study investigating the roles of electronic texts in the humanities projects. The term "netchaining" was coined to describe emerging information and communication practices. Insights from the transliteracy study now add a sense of how community becomes part of netchaining.

The concept of netchaining is based on "chaining" as a well-established form of identifying information sources by following references from one document to another. Netchaining refers to online interactions in which hyperlinks from academic and nonacademic online sources lead to new information, or motivate a new search or online communication. The following main reasons for netchaining activities including other people were identified in the previous publications (Sukovic, 2008, 2011):

- **To find information**
  Example: Asking the author of an electronic poem about technical details, or asking a question and inviting the person to take part in a conference on the topic of common interest.

- **To aid access to a physical collection**
  Example: Using online contact details to ask questions about the collection, sometimes to include information in a grant application and organize a trip to the physical collection.
- **To confirm information**
  Example: Posting a question on a mailing list or contacting the author if information did not appear reliable and there were no readily available alternative sources.
- **For the purposes of current awareness**
  Example: Connecting with online networks and communicating with people as part of general awareness and information monitoring.

Although communication is not necessarily part of netchaining, it is often included in information activities. The purpose of communication may easily change, so communication to find information, for example, may lead to a whole range of networking opportunities.

Subsequent data-gathering enhanced my initial understanding of netchaining and provided evidence for another aspect of netchaining—**being part of the community**. All reasons for participating in or initiating netchaining activities involving other people are presented in Table 3.1.

Students who work as part of a group and know each other's interests and challenges forward relevant information to group members when they come across something useful. It may require little effort to share information online or some effort to include other people's information needs in searching online. The HoAS team, for example, worked with a sense of a broader community. Researchers would answer questions from the public as part of their contribution to the community, but it would be also a way of getting to know people, connect with the community, and receive valuable information. Information skills become intertwined with communication and interpersonal skills. In netchaining, navigating an information landscape in a truly transliterate manner requires an ability to construct an effective search, recognize trustworthy information, and communicate with people, often in unexpected ways. An ability to use acceptable social practices and to incorporate understanding of subtle communication clues in information chains becomes part of participating in information environments. Netchaining and working with other people are often indistinguishable in transliterate ways of working.

3.2.3 Presenting work

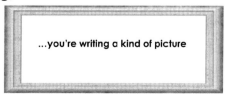

...you're writing a kind of picture

Participant 16/1

Unlike research and creation, which are done with a degree of privacy, any presentation of work is an act of public communication with a wider audience. Presented work is usually in stable forms. Even temporally bound performances often leave

Table 3.1 **Reasons for initiating or participating in netchaining activities involving other people**

Reasons for netchaining	Netchaining activities
To find information	
• Interested in further information about a document • To confirm detail(s) from e-text • If information is crucial • If author's authority could not be discounted • Interested in technical details of electronic literature • If curious	• Contacted a person who may know • Looked up author's website • Made a note for future use • Contacted the responsible person and asked question(s) • Connected that person into own network, invited to a conference
To aid access to a physical collection	
• To confirm details about a collection • To arrange a visit to an archive	• Contacted archivist listed on the website
To confirm information	
• When worried about trustworthiness of a document	• Posted a question to a discussion list contacted the responsible person
For current awareness	
• Coming across new work, wondering what other people do	• Contacted the author • Initiated online discussion about the type of work people are doing • Contacted people outside the discussion list
To be part of a community	
• To assist a known or unknown community member • To seek information or advice • To be in touch	• Offered needed information • Asked questions of community members

Published in Sukovic (2008, 2011). 'To be part of a community' is added here.

material traces in forms of documents, recordings and images. As most people put a great deal of conscious thought into presentation, it is often easier to discuss and provide evidence for the decision-making processes leading to final products. Presentation of one's work is a form of communication, so it always relates to the social context. Although the focus in this section is on issues of genres and participatory audience, as these define presentation decisions, the following discussions are underpinned by the awareness that any presentation of work is a social act. As indicated in Fig. 3.4, creativity is a particular prominent element of transliteracy at this stage.

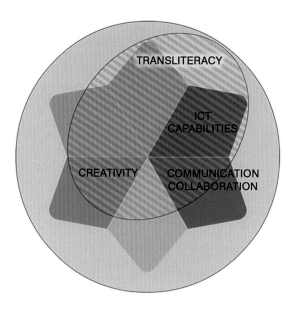

Figure 3.4 Presenting work.

3.2.3.1 Genres: understanding, multimodality, and change

Transliterate ways of working lead the presenter to think about presentation options and the possibility of combining different genres, modes, tones, and technologies. Remixing was a prominent metaphor used by several academics to describe interactions with a variety of resource materials as both a form of exploration and communication of results. Transliterate practices lead to a heightened awareness of different forms of expression, media, and modalities and to a gradual change of traditional genres.

> *A lot of cultural work now . . . is formed out of this process of mixing and remixing, of taking existing artefacts, existing portions of things and not stealing them so much, but putting them into novel combinations and layering them. (U Participant 6/2)*
>
> *It's more about readily remixing all the various texts that I had at my disposal. I think of the artist more as a medium than an instrument. It's like a DJ who has a stack of records that they mix in a live performance, so I do that with my virtual stack of writing, it's just spinning and sampling from and coming up with the essay, with the narrative construction around this innovative path. (U Participant 15/1)*

Understanding of genres and media
Time and time again, I heard and observed how people had started with an intention to produce the output in a traditional form—a talk, a poster, or a Power Point

presentation at school; a traditional conference paper, academic article, or book at universities—only to realize at some point that these formats could not do justice to the ideas they wanted to communicate. In some instances, participants would change or expand their output to include works in less traditional forms; in many other instances, they would just reflect on the inadequacies of well-established genres, which they would still use to meet requirements or follow established academic practices.

Regardless of what the final product was, a better understanding of genres and formats emerged from thinking about different ways of presenting the results of transliterate explorations. Multimodality becomes an important aspect of transliterate presentations, but even subtle shifts in established ways of writing and presenting lead to changing genres and formats.

In most instances, participants are in largely uncharted territory, which sharpens their awareness of the research process and possibilities of different forms of expression. Participant 13/1 explained how he moved between different formats and technologies without anxiety, but with a heightened awareness of different encounters: "To encounter a book and to think in relation to a book or to encounter a printed photograph on photographic paper in your hands is a different encounter from encountering a photograph digitized on the screen." When asked how they were different, he answered, "The way the light plays off the surface, what your eye is drawn to, what thoughts and feelings come to you in response to the image in those different circumstances." Participant 15/1 worked in the area of new media. Experimentation with technologies and genres was at the core of his work. He commented on how he experimented "with all these different kinds of writing styles so I'm not limited to one particular style, but at the same time, I am self-aware of when I'm getting into what I think of as more 'spontaneous writer in a poetic mode', creative writing mode, and when I'm getting into a more academic mode."

High school students and academics alike discussed the connection between the content and different genres, media, and modalities. For many academics, the choice of outcomes corresponded to the materials and practices they used during their research as they explored different ways of working with evidence. For example, Participant 3/1 decided that outputs of a collaborative project would be a monograph, reports, practical guidelines, and a community-based website, closely reflecting resources and techniques used in the study. A high school student commented on how she had experience with making videos, but digital stories enabled a different sort of expression: "[W]ith digital stories I can be a lot more dramatic. And, quite philosophical with digital stories... The videos that we make, they're usually like music videos or ads or like five minute movies about... fiction" (HS N.). Another student explained how adoption of a blog as a genre solved her writing problem as it was a better fit for the content of her digital story. Many students commented on various techniques they tried and effects they produced.

The construction of the final product is usually intertwined with working with materials and the process of sense-making, although it could be a result of the final identification of key ideas that the author wishes to communicate. Students in the *Truth and Reality* project discussed whether forms of presentation should be considered early in the process. Some commented that they could not consider presentation without knowing its content. Others had a different view. One student regretted that she did not decide earlier about the presentation, so she could have a more focused approach to collecting relevant pieces of information to use in the final stages. Another student who used artistic portraits to look into the construction of an artist's identity felt she made a breakthrough in her project when she decided how she was going to present her ideas.

The information and creation process often go hand in hand. Early decisions about presentation may inform and guide the research process, particularly for creative people and those who work comfortably in multimodal ways, common in transliteracy.

Multimodality

Interaction with a variety of media motivates researchers interested in expressing ideas by using multimedia to think about integrating some of them in the final stages of their work. Participant 2/2 explained some elaborate techniques of working with textual and audio files and how she would like to use them to communicate her ideas:

> And then, when I have come to give conference papers, to actually take up pieces
> and put them together is actually really productive in thinking things through, that
> sort of cut and paste and, hearing the transitions in the speaking styles. If you take
> out one minute from a show from 1950 and juxtapose it to something from 1960,
> you really hear it changes. And so, that's sort of mixing and matching.

Multimedia is more suitable for certain types of ideas, which do not fit easily into traditional academic arguments and genres. Participant 6/2 commented on the decision to create two types of output for different strands of research results. A creative database was developed to present important but inconclusive research material, while results for which the researcher had the final interpretation were seen as suitable for a book:

> This is extremely moving and important material, it's extremely narrative, but it's
> inconclusive. You'll never put a kind of an "Amen" to all of this, it will always be
> stimulating possible narratives. Therefore, in order to attend to or bear witness
> to that quality of the material, I need to make something which is organized and
> authored and persuasive, but endless and inconclusive. And explicitly inclusive,
> so that leads me to think, "Oh, that needs to be computationally driven."

Writing is also influenced by a sense of multimodality. A student chose text for her digital story from several pieces of her writing because it was suitable to be combined with visuals. Another student explained how she realized she needed to change her writing to complement rather than describe pictures in her digital story. Participant 16/1 showed examples from her academic book to demonstrate how electronic text, particularly e-poetry, changed the way she wrote. Meaning is expressed by using less text and more visual techniques. Blocks of text are presented side by side and fonts are changed, for example, to produce certain effects for a reader.

This literary scholar explained how she thought "of screenfuls of writing" when she wrote her creative and academic work:

> You think of writing in a spatial way, so to some degree . . . **you're writing a kind of picture**. I mean, this has been done, of course, on the page with things like concrete poetry and visual poetry, that existed far long before the Internet, but . . . I think it's really brought to the fore a lot. So you . . . can start at any point and you think of people reading that they might make any kind of connection. And also, of course, the main thing about it is that it's kinetic and . . . that you think about what can happen when a word goes from one point, moves from one point of the screen to another point in the screen.
>
> U Participant 16/1, emphasis by SS

Change of genres

Once people start experimenting with technologies, styles, and techniques, changes of genres are inevitable. Digital stories typically consist of images, usually photographs, voice, and music used for narration. In several years of iTell, the task given to students as a general direction remained the same—students were asked to make a digital recreation of an oral story or create a response to a written fictional story. Their responses, however, branched out to incorporate a range of styles, techniques, and subgenres. Students produced fictional stories, documentaries combined with personal memories, and many variations on storytelling and poetry, in addition to closer responses to the initial task. Stories were told in one, two, or many voices. Beside standard techniques of using still images, they used animation, stop motion, and photographs of acted scenes with costumes, masks, and objects especially made for their story. A student discussed how experience in iTell stimulated her creativity and mentioned an example of mixing films and digital stories at home: "I would have . . . the pictures and stuff and then I'll have writing at the bottom of the screen or I'll record my voice in combination with film and stop motion" (B.).

Academics who studied electronic media commented on the importance of multimodality, coding, and technical skills in new literary genres: "I say it's no longer literature per se, it's something more like net art or internet art or network art. And so it integrates textuality and [narrative] experience but there's also a kind of visual literacy and sonic elements and coding. It complicates the literary" (U Participant 15/1). The same academic commented:

> I saw myself also writing fiction and the fiction becomes theoretical and I saw myself writing artist theory and the artist theory becomes fictional. So all these different kinds of styles and modes of writing were starting to mix into the merge and I decided that I would explore that in a collection of books.

Academic genres such as journal articles and scholarly books, although more stable and resistant to change, are affected by transliteracy. Internet searching and consideration of resources of different provenance and tone emphasized scholars' awareness of different registers in academic writing and, often, inadequacies of traditional academic genres. An academic in literary studies commented on the absence of emotion in academic writing:

> *You're using it for the kind of emotional resonance of it [i.e. information in creative writing] whereas in academic writing you're brought up always ... to kind of get rid of all that stuff. I don't know that's always right to do it, but academic writing has to be coldly, thoughtfully presented in ways that scour off all of the emotional stuff. Whereas in fiction you want it, you deliberately use it to create a reaction for your reader.*
>
> *U Participant 1/2*

The style of factual, strictly rational academic writing based on authoritative sources is unable to capture the richness of research findings for a number of historians. A scholar discussed his historical book and commented on pushing boundaries by including different registers and voices in the book. Elements of a literary style were part of "taking risks" with the book. Another historian commented on his academic education, in which history was seen as an art, not a science and the value of narrative was seen as enriching in communicating history. He observed a shift toward a certain style of analytical academic writing over the years:

> *Some people go in different directions and certainly the academy has tried to push us all in the other direction to write papers all the time. Hmm...which is good, not a bad direction, could lead you online, digitally. But assessors ... are saying this is getting journalistic a bit, not even narrative, they say "journalistic" when I describe a particular scene, which needs traditional skill of narrative. Some upstart young Laconian who is saying, "this is all journalistic style, change your style immediately please—more analysis, less narrative."*
>
> *HoAS, Peter Read*

In his work on the website *A History of Aboriginal Sydney*, he invited authentic and often emotional voices from the community to tell their historical stories. This research approach emphasizes differences in views of historical writing. In Read's opinion, emotion is not only valuable but a necessary part of understanding history, especially history involving traumatic experiences. Multimedia allows the inclusion of voices and layers of information that are usually excluded from academic writing.

Participatory audience

The contemporary audience reads, listens, and watches as the audience has always done, but it has become quite common that people in the audience are invited to participate and respond. Participant 13/1 commented that a book provides a handrail for a reader while "electronic or digital presumes or requires a subjectivity which is more investigative than receptive... You're more delving into the thing, putting together your own thesis in relation to the patterned information that's available, whereas if you're in the presence of a really great book, you tend to allow the author to carry you along." The presenter's/author's interests in exploring the investigative disposition of the audience and in opening conversational spaces are informing decisions about the communication of research results. The selection of interactive digital forms to present research results is based on understanding that the author will not present a definitive authorial view.

A broad online audience and the expectation that the audience will determine the extent of engagement presents its challenges in establishing an appropriate style:

> *I was beginning to think, in terms of the actual text, of having to compress it into the language that was readable by a wide range of students, anything from Year 8 [at high school] to 3rd year university and even PhD. So trying to pitch to the audience that broad was a challenge. But I veered away from too complex language. And, I think, that was the right decision. Peter agreed with that. He realised that our biggest audience would be at school and universities. It's a challenge—you take a large amount of historical documentation and you want to quote large amounts from it. But, if it ends up going into pages and pages, you know that your reader will possibly not read it.*
>
> HoAS, Julie Janson

Similarly to the online presentation of research, interactivity embedded in live presentations is based on the premise that the audience will want to explore ideas along a constructed path. Many students who presented at the *Truth and Reality* expo decided to follow suggestions made in class and think of interactive ways of presenting. Participation in peers' activities was a valuable learning opportunity and student observations of the audience were an extension of their learning. For the audience, activities and the presentation of many different approaches were ways of constructing their own understandings of the topic. The participatory audience then becomes an actor in the research process, influencing not only the presentation choices but also a developing understanding of the topic. This became apparent as students discussed how audience reactions became part of their developing understanding of the open-endedness of their topic and presentation outcomes.

What constitutes transliteracy? Summary

- **Working with a multiplicity of resources**: Interaction with a multiplicity of resources with different characteristics by using a range of media technologies and techniques to open new lines of investigation and creative approaches. Working with resources by using a range of techniques and technologies, often constructing meaning by connecting disparate information and ideas
- **Working with others**: Communicating and collaborating with different people in person and via digital media across social groupings, including participation in netchaining
- **Presenting results** of one's own work by incorporating different tones, voices, modalities, formats, and genres.

3.3 Experience

Experience of transliterate ways of working is quite novel for teenagers and academics alike. Even academics specializing in new media describe their work and personal experience as experimentation with something new and largely unknown. In this section, the focus is on participants' experiences, perceptions, and thoughts to answer the second research question, "How do participants experience transliteracy?" Study results are first presented in relation to participants' engagement, emotions, and responses to creative experiences. A sense of individuality is described under the heading *In one's own voice* (see Section 3.3.2), while the final section deals with experiences of transliteracy in relation to protocols, analog materials, and technology.

3.3.1 Engagement and emotional responses

It was always on my mind in a way, at the back of my mind thinking, "What I can do next week and the week after?"

HS, Enrichment

Engagement is a critically important aspect of learning and any sustained intellectual work. Academics are expected to be immersed in their research, so issues of engagement were not systematically investigated other than in relation to participants' experiences with e-texts and digital media. Since it is often an issue in the regular classroom, engagement was carefully monitored in the high school setting. Questions about enjoyment were included in all student surveys and interviews.

"Fun" is probably the word most frequently used by students in relation to transliteracy, especially outside regular classrooms. Surveys of students in iTell and LevelUp showed that their enjoyment in these workshops was on a par with the enjoyment of their favorite subject and extracurricular activities. All students in these workshops agreed or strongly agreed with general statements about interest and enjoyment during the programs. Fig. 3.5, for example, shows responses regarding enjoyment of particular aspects of iTell indicated by numbers corresponding to the four point Likert scale, with "4" as the highest value. Even students who were disengaged in regular classes enjoyed workshops. A relatively large group of students was included in iTell by the school to try an alternative approach with these consistently disengaged students. Most of them enjoyed iTell and produced work of good quality. A talented, but rebellious student, O., who was disengaged from almost all school activities at the time, commented about iTell: "It turned out to be fun in the end."

Gifted and talented students selected for the Enrichment classes and French students who worked in regular classes expressed more mixed feelings. The majority enjoyed transliteracy projects, but there were issues which clouded their sense of enjoyment. The group of gifted students in the Enrichment program expressed feelings of anxiety before the final expo, a fair-style presentation for the families and teachers lasting a couple of hours. Issues related to the organization of their work

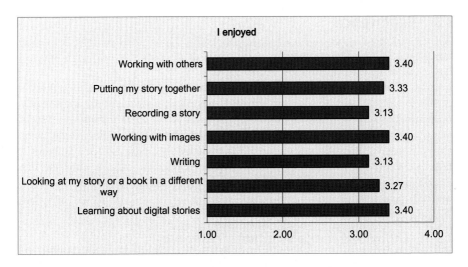

Figure 3.5 iTell survey: enjoyment in activities.

and performance had a negative impact on their enjoyment, especially in the final stages of the project when preparations for the expo coincided with yearly examinations. The expo itself, however, was mentioned as one of the most enjoyable parts of the project as students felt free to explore and did not feel any pressure because their work was already completed. Students in the French class were frustrated by the technology, which did not work smoothly. The class had lost some lessons, so there was not sufficient time to assist students who struggled with the app Aurasma. Their teacher commented on some students being "out of their comfort zone," which is probably an important reason why a couple of them expressed a sense of anxiety about classroom novelties.

Working with or alongside peers in a collaborative manner helped students to maintain interest and learn from each other, but also triggered a range of emotional responses. Most participants mentioned a sense of connection and personal support as enjoyable and helpful in dealing with challenging tasks. Some negative thoughts and feelings were mentioned as well. For many students, being with a mixed age group of less familiar faces was a cause for initial insecurity or even anxiety. Learning from peers sometimes meant less favorable comparisons, which would evoke personal insecurities. That was an issue in some iTell groups when high achieving students worked alongside those who struggled at school. A student in iTell commented, "It's not my thing. I don't read books, I don't do anything on the computer that's all technical and smart like that" (HS U.). This comment was made as part of a focus group discussion in which students were comparing themselves with some high achieving students in the workshop. In French classes, students said they learned a lot by being immersed in conversations with each other and watching each other's videos. A student also commented on how she "got worked up and stopped listening" when other students used sophisticated French, which made them hard to understand. These types of reaction are important indicators of areas for student development considering that transliteracy requires an ability to participate in diverse networks.

Most negative feelings were reportedly replaced by a sense of achievement and new connections over a period of time. A junior student described her feelings in iTell workshops in the following way:

> *As soon as I saw a massive group I was like, "Oh, I don't know, I don't know many of these girls, I might just..." Probably it was going to be just Year 8s, 9s, 10s everyone in their little groups. But then some people left and some people came back, we all got to know one another. Like, I would've never known Lucy. But now, when I see her, I am like, "Stop Lus" [laughs happily]. I didn't feel we were all like in our own little groups, year groups. We were all talking to each other and it was so much fun.*
>
> *HS, J.*

Creativity was often mentioned as a prominent and very enjoyable aspect of transliteracy workshops and classes. The French class chose creativity after "working with peers" as a main contributor to their learning. A student in the Enrichment class engaged fully with the topic once we found a way to include her interest in visual arts. Congruence with personal interests and goals, especially flexibility in defining individual projects to include student artistic talents and interests, was another bonus for the Enrichment classes. Responses to the statement "I had opportunities to be creative" were indicated on the Likert scale with "4" as the maximum value (Fig. 3.6). Students in the French class did not have this question in the survey.

A sense of exploration was an important contributor to positive feelings for both students and academics. When historian Peter Read started working on the HoAS

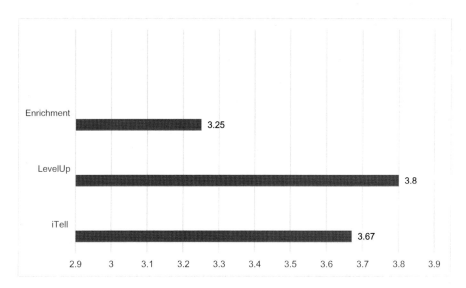

Figure 3.6 Responses to the statement "I had opportunities to be creative."

website, he "thought it was an exciting adventure." Students in the Enrichment class mentioned how they were more excited about the *Truth and Reality* project than about going to the normal class. One student discussed how she felt fulfilled and another added: "When I was looking forward to it, it was 'What else can I research?' It was always on my mind in a way, at the back of my mind thinking, 'What I can do next week and the week after?'—trying to plan it all out."

Exploration of a wide range of materials contributed to enjoyment and engagement, but it was also seen as a source of confusion and stress. Students in the Enrichment class emphasized how they enjoyed the exploration of a wide range of relevant resources provided in the library. Similarly, an academic commented:

> *And with something like the maps, for example, where you've got the parish maps,*
> *involve so many layers of handwritten changes, it's really critical—and to have*
> *access to those at home, any time of the day or night, is just magic.*
>
> *U Participant 3/1, emphasis by SS*

Another academic commented on an overwhelming abundance of relevant resources and added: "I feel like it's a baptism of fire for me. I'm only just beginning to learn how to measure and manage all of these electronic possibilities" (U Participant 7/1).

Online interactions can be very useful and enjoyable, but they can be also perceived as draining. One of the students in iTell commented on how long searches for suitable images and music were boring and frustrating. An academic found short bursts of searching throughout the day in the office "stressful and spasmodic." Interactions with multimedia on websites, on the other hand, can contribute to a sense of engagement by including senses: "I guess it's the cross-media or convergent media model . . . it's interactive, you click on something here. **It changes your sense of time** as well because when you hear something, old audio, you often feel like you're really back in that time" (U Participant 2/2, emphasis by SS).

Space and time were repeatedly mentioned as important aspects of feeling connected with work. Many academics were taking reading home so they could feel comfortable and focused. The library was frequently mentioned as a place conducive to doing focused work. Participant 1/2, for example, commented on the pleasures of working in the library and a sense that walking through the library door signifies accessing research space. High school students stressed how much they loved working in the library with its pleasant ambience, more relaxed sitting arrangements and readily available resources. In all transliteracy projects, students felt they benefited when longer periods in the library were available, as they provided the right space and time for engaging work.

3.3.2   In one's own voice

> *. . .it's mainly just who I am*
>
> *U Participant 15/1*

A perception and the presence of individual voices are reinforced in transliterate projects and interactions, through either the act of creation or the presentation of individual work. Student M. commented on her experience with digital storytelling: "I don't really like speaking that much so that was kind of just a bit more personal... I guess putting your own voice to it and sometimes that can be a bit hard." She felt a sense of accomplishment that she did that and finally felt comfortable with her own voice. Another student found that her individual *Truth and Reality* project made her focus on her own ideas:

> *It [the project] kinda taught me you can't really - not that I was relying on other people, but whenever I came to class I'd be more interested in listening to other people's ideas and putting my own in. So when I did the project, putting my ideas in was the main thing I had to focus on.*

Experimentation with technologies and genres led some students to discover new talents and interests. A junior student who experimented with filming and digital storytelling techniques to create an original story won a prestigious price at a school film festival in a competition with senior students. The whole experience of participating in iTell and her subsequent success made her decide that she wanted to become a director.

Multiplicity of voices promotes a sense of multifarious knowledge. Interviews with the Indigenous community published on the HoAS website brought forward voices of people who rarely or never had a chance to speak publicly about their own memories and historical knowledge. A project team member commented: "I think it's great because I think we so often want to give some kind of overarching narrative that gives some containment and makes it safer or brings everyone together in some way. [We are] having everybody just say 'this is my truth'" (HoAS, Chantal Jackson). A number of students in the Enrichment project commented on how class discussions in which there was no right and wrong answer, and presentation activities in which the audience showed their understanding of an issue at hand, made them understand other people's perspectives better.

A multiplicity of online voices and an abundance of information can make it difficult to establish one's own voice as an academic. A scholar commented on how he always writes what he thinks first and encourages his doctoral students to do the same:

> *It prevents me from being disheartened because in my field there is so much done, there are so many things being done, it can be incredibly disheartening. To a PhD student...it would be, it's terrible.*
>
> *U Participant 14/1*

On the other hand, being part of this multiplicity of voices is perceived as part of an academic identity by some scholars. When asked about the importance of online connections and whether "being part of that whole environment and network of people helps you to get what you're after," Participant 15/1 answered, "Totally. I mean it's mainly just who I am."

3.3.3   Technology and protocols

When we were given a choice of presenting by using anything, whatever technology that we needed to use, it stretched us to use, and not just sticking in our comfort zone, to think outside the box and we thought of something creative

HS, Enrichment

Paper, pens, books, tapes, computers, mobile devices, and software are all key players in transliteracy, in the sense of Latour's Actor-Network Theory (Latour, 2005). Thoughts, feelings, and attitudes to these technologies and the way they are used are significant in identifying and understanding transliteracy. Participants in the study discussed their thoughts and emotions related to the use of technology in a way that can be related to their experience. It was mainly students who talked about their thoughts and feelings related to digital technology, while academics talked about protocols and what different interactions contributed to their research.

Students in digital storytelling and coding workshops expressed predominantly positive thoughts and feelings about technology. In iTell, students commented on how putting a digital story together was "really cool" or "these were my favorite parts." French students enjoyed using Edmodo, with interactions similar to those possible on Facebook, as they were able to be in touch with the class and learn from each other in an informal way. Most students enjoyed the creation of videos, especially when they did not find this technology challenging.

Issues with technology arose when it did not work as expected. One student in iTell struggled initially with transition from Mac to PC computers. Difficulties in using the app Aurasma were a source of considerable frustration for the French class. In the following discussion in the focus group, the students reflected on their dealings with technology:

SS: Are you learning something when things are not working?
Student 1: How to deal with frustration with technology.
SS: How did you deal with that frustration?
Student 1: Not very well.
Student 2: Harder to learn what you are supposed to learn when you are dealing with technology and frustration of technology not working.
Student 3: I think it's good. Creative things are fun. You are learning as you are doing. I learn from doing things. Writing things down 50 times wouldn't make me learn it.

Aurasma, which frustrated many students in the French class, was on offer to the Enrichment class. One student used it very successfully and creatively. She commented on how she wanted to try something new: "When we were given a choice of presenting by using anything, whatever technology that we needed to use, it stretched us to use and not just sticking in our comfort zone, to think outside the box and thought of something creative."

Working with and learning about technology is easier in a collaborative group in which students and educators (librarians, in this case) work together. For shy or introverted students, it creates a supportive environment in which they can ask questions. A student discussed valuable skills she gained in iTell:

> *First of all, the skills that we learned like the technology skills. Those were really good because even though we do need to use them a lot more in class, we don't really get a lot of time to learn about it and teachers often don't really know a lot about it either. And then also, I think, being able to talk to other people and get other ideas from people, because a lot of the time I find that I just work by myself and if I'm not sure I try to work it out by myself and I often don't ask questions and ask other people.*
>
> *HS M.*

Academics discussed how their thought processes may change in interaction with digital and analog technologies. Analog materials were valued by researchers who exhibited elaborate transliterate behaviors, as they supported serendipitous discoveries and a sense of connection with the content. Even for scholars with considerable experience of the innovative use of digital technology, there is a time and place for research with analog materials and technology.

An important issue for some scholars is a sense of attachment to traditional research processes, which they often see as a generational issue. Teenagers, however, also expressed their enjoyment of books as physical objects and often a preference for working with analog materials. This preference is often a result of circumstances. The assumption of many academics that younger generations are more inclined and adapted to use digital technology in their work was not supported by the evidence. Teenagers and academics both enjoy or avoid certain technologies depending on circumstances. Accepting one's own or someone else's challenge to try something new often results in productive discoveries and a sense of achievement.

An academic discussed a sense of alienation in computer-driven information retrieval:

I guess it's feeling like you went and found that rather than the database found it for you [laughs]. You know, you actually have a relationship to it by finding it. And maybe using index or something but you actually went, made the step to find the object whereas in an electronic version it's all the same. The file, the mp3 file, has within it the metatext, which tells you where it is, just magically comes up.

SS: So it's not yours in a way. It alienates the process. Is it what you are saying?

The machine has made the decision about bringing it to you based on what you've asked the machine to give to you rather than you matching up information with themes that might be best. (U Participant 2/2)

(Continued)

(cont'd)

Connection between the development of ideas and technology was expressed in the following way:

I'm terrified by these things and I regard myself as terribly—I mean... when I start writing an article or start on a book or even if it's a short story or something non-academic, I start by sharpening a pencil with a penknife and start writing in pencil. And then move on to my fountain pen. And then when I'm comfortable with what I'm doing, I then move onto the computer. It's a rite of passage... If I can't get onto the fountain pen stage, I know it won't get onto the computer stage... I have noticed over the last few years that the time from moving from sharpening the pencil, which is really clearing time for myself, to getting onto the computer is getting shorter and shorter. (U Participant 6/1)

Some academics assume that younger generations have a significantly different attitude to research with technology:

I think anyone over 45 or 50, you probably went through humanities—stacks, essays, research, all the kind of traditional. And that is the love-hate thing, you know, the passion in lots of ways around process as much as outcome. And if you're young and you grew up with the Internet, you probably have got a very different attitude to it. I think... the point of your life [when you are] entering new way of research to some extent governs how you feel about it. I love it, I think the Internet's great, I use it and I like using it but I always feel there's a kind of generational, cultural thing around it that probably someone much younger, like my students, don't have at all. (U Participant 1/2)

How do participants experience transliteracy? Summary
- Heightened classroom engagement, a sense of fun and particularly positive response to opportunities to work creatively
- Benefits of learning with and from peers
- Discovery of "own voice"
- Some negative feelings associated with information overload, frustration of dealing with technology, and, for teenagers, working with peers
- Need for digital and analog technologies with no evidence of major generational differences in preference.

3.4 Contribution to learning and knowledge production

What it means and how it feels to work in transliterate ways have been the focus of this chapter so far. The next question is "How does transliteracy contribute to participants' learning and knowledge production?" In this section, the first set of answers is about multiple ways of knowing and communicating: working in different modes and media, considering a range of tones and voices, and communicating in different ways and through multiple channels. The second set of answers concerns the contributions of transliteracy to learning, including the evidence of learning gains and the ways in which "learning across" occurs.

3.4.1 Multiple ways of knowing and communicating

It means any Aboriginal person in Australia, can click on that website and find an elder or a person who is talking about their history. And it hasn't been filtered to an historian's opinion. It's right from the horse's mouth... And there was an opportunity to bear witness to their lives. That's what makes it such a magical and important website. And when I introduce people to it and they have a look, they ring me up and say, "Oh, my God, that was extraordinary. I stayed on it all night looking at all these stories..."

HoAS, Julie Janson

Sense-making is a complex process. Transliterate ways of working bring new elements into this complexity—new voices, new sensibilities based on multimodal experiences, and a broadened perception of communication options. Learning and knowledge development happens while crossing traditionally segregated knowledge fields.

3.4.1.1 Modes and media

Once opportunities for transliterate ways of working are created, it is interesting to observe how transliteracy takes on a life of its own. Given the opportunity, visual people start telling a story by drawing pictures with minimal or no text, or using color extensively in notes. Listening to music while working can aid engagement and creativity, and different senses contribute to learning and understanding. Multisensory perception entails uncovering layers of information, normally absent from textual sources. Some participants described the importance of learning from nonverbal clues and through the body.

A HoAS team member discussed the value of using videos rather than text to record community memories:

Text is more removed. And I love text, I love reading and I love reading stories, but it's that different thing. You can get a felt sense of somebody [from videos]. And somebody who is not necessarily very articulate, you can see the emotions going over their face. So you get a whole world of information you wouldn't get otherwise. So I think it's really good from that perspective. [HoAS, Chantal Jackson]

Nondiscursive knowledge is enhanced in digital environments:

And multisensory and also temporarily, like, emerging and losing in time, emerging and disappearing in time. That's the other thing ...what the [title of the

(Continued)

(cont'd)

researcher's digital work] is trying to explore in a way... that tip of the tongue sensation in a way that "Uh! Just for a moment I knew something and then it went away." And, that doesn't mean therefore it was useless knowledge, it actually was just an intense momentary way of knowing. And, I think dancers and musicians know that very well...It's not discursive knowledge, but it's knowledge of some kind. And it's knowledge that isn't mystical, it's knowledge that is trained and rigorously developed and it's very disciplined. **It's just different knowledge, I think, from textual knowledge. I find that very exciting that the electronic world is bringing ... that way of knowing into experience more thoroughly or more plentifully or to more people.** *(U Participant 6/2, emphasis by SS)*

Participants commented on their heightened awareness of different modes and media as they influence their work. Some academics said they were not conscious of how their experience with different arts and media shaped their work and digital interactions for some time, but it was increasingly becoming part of their thinking, theorizing, and writing. High school students commented on their new awareness of information coming from different senses and how it is expressed. A junior student discussed her writing for a digital story:

It makes it easier with the pictures. Cos in my stories I am always like "and Bubbler with his yellow pants and blue top" but if you have a photo of it, you don't have to say that. Cos everyone will see it while they are visualizing in their head what I am saying.

HS N.

A similar idea was expressed by an academic who explained combinations of visual elements with text and the sound of words to create certain experiences for the reader. This academic commented:

Well, I have a whole chapter which is on writing and performance and, for instance, it has a section on sonic poetry and there sonic poetry is about balancing the sound [with the senses] of words and also maybe bringing words together with music. So it's, to some degree it's bringing together different systems of meaning. It's bringing together music as a system and writing as a system and it's saying that kind of logical sense isn't everything, that there's the sound to the words and to the way we immerse ourselves in text. ... [A]nd I think the whole book's a bit like that, it's not just the logical meanings of the words, there's a lot more to writing than that.

U Participant 16/1

Academics stressed that different modes and media were used to create certain effects well before the development of digital technology. They thought, however, that the technology had offered many new opportunities and brought new qualities into their work, especially in providing means for building layered artefacts.

3.4.1.2 Tones and voices

Interactions with a range of materials bring different tones and types of knowledge into one's field of awareness. Particularly significant are online interactions in which a range of voices mix and merge. A scholar who studied contemporary religious movements commented on the value of different tones and perspectives encountered on discussion forums about extraterrestrial life, advertisements for trips to places of religious significance and academic work about popular phenomena. Even commitment to one particular register is based on an awareness of other options and judgment about their relevance, appropriateness, and accessibility. Academics in the study discussed issues of authority and what the presence of different voices, tones, and registers means for scholarship. A study participant commented that contemporary openness to a multiplicity of voices arises from the changing sense of authority:

> *That people are no longer basically trustful of single authoritative disposition, single authoritative discourse, they want to be able to cross reference, cross check, find a secondary opinion, etc etc, and come to their own belief rather than just accept an authorised view. And that, I think, is partly to do with the amount of change or the amount of instability or the amount of contradictory or multifarious belief systems that everyone encounters now in their everyday life. So these cultural forms have grown up as people have needed them.*
>
> *U Participant 13/1*

Topics and sources, which have not been traditionally regarded as appropriate for scholarly investigation, are considered valuable when scholars are willing to research across domains and protocols. Participant 9/1, who works in the field of religious studies, commented on a project examining a particular occurrence of Virgin Mary apparitions, which attracted a great deal of public attention at the time. This project was based mainly on public responses to the phenomenon, connecting theoretical and historical knowledge with the news reports. The participant commented on how the willingness to study new topics is based on the growing awareness that any research is provisional, so scholars are more open to working with different sources. The sense of a team, playing a constantly developing game in which every "player carries the ball for a while" is present in this approach to research:

> *And nowadays, that provisionality is made more obvious by the greater availability or multitudinous nature of material. So anything you say is just a provisional statement about something. I think it's very funny. And when I wrote the Virgin Mary article, the two referees from the journal, one of them sent back a "no," saying every source in this is a newspaper or magazine article or television documentary, it's not proper academic work. And the other one said "cutting edge, deeply original, should be published". It's now been cited by at least half a dozen*

other people who are now working on these apparitions of the Virgin Mary ... it's
weeping statues in Rockingham in Western Australia and toasted cheese
sandwiches on eBay and all that sort of stuff. But that's really cool, that's kind of
nice that you've become part of kind of spinning the industry, you just have
something and then somebody else picks up—like the ball in football, somebody
else picks it up and runs with it and it goes off and has a life of its own.

U Participant 9/1

With new technologies, it is relatively easy to bring authentic new voices into
academic research by recording them and publishing online. This, however, requires
an ability to work across cultures and protocols. When historians make authentic
voices available as part of their research output, they bring the emotion and difference in opinions sharply into focus. A member of the HoAS team commented on
how short videos convey meaning "much better than reading an analysis and someone's opinion about how difficult it was for Aboriginal people."

All that stuff, it kind of gives that sense of bitsy-pieceness, of fragmentation within
community as well as communities trying to come together. I think it is very real,
but because people are just being themselves and they are just short videos, you
see all these bits and pieces. There are underlying themes, they do unify it. It's not
like you are left with this kind of messy confusion that doesn't even make sense...
And you start to get a sense of what are the pressures, what are the stark
experiences that are making people be as they are here and what are they actually
struggling with to try to find their way. And, of course, you can see why everybody
has got a different take. This person was given traditional knowledge, this person
found out when they were 30 that they were Aboriginal, so everyone is having a
different take. So to me it all made sense.

HoAS, Chantal Jackson

The interviewing style used by the HoAS team to bring forward individual
experiences requires a form of cultural crossing as the researcher is adopting the
communication style of the community. An Indigenous researcher on the team commented: "Sharing information rather than direct questioning. It's that thing like
'I have to cut you in half and find out what you've got and take it away' ... Using
this gentler approach, just slowly gaining the confidence of person over half an
hour so they begin to unburden themselves" (HoAS Julie Janson).

The researcher's willingness and ability to move across cultural boundaries to
bring into focus community voices enriches and broadens mainstream knowledge,
on one hand. On the other hand, information sharing is powerful for the community
as a way of discovering its own past and opening opportunities for connection and
healing. Understanding one's history may lead to important personal and community outcomes, as was the case with a team member who found evidence of her
own Aboriginality, or a small community which prepared a land claim submission
on the basis of historical data they discovered.

Transliteracy opens conversational spaces for many voices absent from the public discourse. While digital oral histories have existed for a while, the HoAS

website provides unique historical records about Indigenous people in a large Australian city, contributing to academic research, community interest, and learning at school, while opening opportunities for a data comparison by any researcher across the globe.

In the classroom, a shift away from the authority of the teacher opens space for student-centered learning, which includes learning from peers and other people. For French students, the use of videos meant that every girl in the class could see and listen to other girls' creations in French and learn from them. The French teacher commented that the students have already used a range of technologies for input, "but not so much for output."

> *The kids become the author of something that is available to a bigger variety of people rather than just using the exercise book and me marking it and giving it back. So to use the Edmodo website where everyone can see what others are writing, thereby having an element of peer checking, or 'bagging, borrowing and stealing' as I like to call it.*
>
> *HS French teacher*

Publishing videos online makes "the idea that there is a big audience" an important motivation to strive for one's best performance. Even the act of sharing video recordings with the class changes the focus from the teacher to a broader audience. Students in the Enrichment program also appreciated opportunities to learn from one another, in addition to valuable interactions with the audience. A student commented about the expo:

> *I saw ideas I haven't even thought about. When you see everyone else's [it] makes you realise there are so many different ways you can present. And we have this knowledge for the future assignments and for anything in any other subjects. We know more ideas to present as well just from seeing what other people have done.*

Another student investigated issues of truth and reality by looking into portraits and self-portraits. She provided some activities for the audience. As people did not respond as expected, it made her think and consider how every person has a different perspective, adding another layer to her thinking about the topic.

The HoAS team about the value of different and authentic voices:

It means any Aboriginal person in Australia, can click on that website and find an elder or a person who is talking about their history. And it hasn't been filtered to an historian's opinion. It's right from the horse's mouth. And I think it was really important to Peter and certainly to the people we interviewed. And there was an opportunity to bear witness to their lives. That's what makes it such a magical and important website. And when I introduce people to it and they have a look, they ring me up and say, "Oh, my God, that was extraordinary. I stayed on it all night

(Continued)

(cont'd)

looking at all these stories and the way it was easy to interact and between the different sections and the galleries and video galleries". And I had nothing but very excited feedback from Aboriginal community people. (HoAS, Julie Janson)

All that wonderful language and a view of the country, how it was created, the poetic imaginative view of how things worked. We don't know even what it was, we didn't know even subsections of Sydney until 1980s. So that sense of what's been lost. And another feeling I had—something you may like to communicate now—but, that's the point, it's not just a personal vehicle, it's something different, it's not just writing a book. (HoAS, Peter Read)

Read commented on a memorable trip with an Indigenous fellow-academic when he learned a lot about the Aboriginal history of Sydney from a traditional perspective:

And his stories of how Sydney was created and the ceremonies that were being carried out for young women's education, young men's education, where they stopped, where the smoke was...That's absolute magic to me. And that's what really inspires me. When I listen to Dennis, he is a living treasure and having so much traditional education, I know now where he got it from. (HoAS, Peter Read)

3.4.1.3 Communication

Communication in new ways, getting in touch with a wider audience and an ability to communicate different content and meanings are some of the outcomes achieved through transliteracy. For high school students, the real meaning of learning a language becomes more clearly obvious as they record their conversations and publish them online. For students in iTell and a historian, the use of digital means opens novel and useful ways of communicating.

The beauty of this whole transliteracy thing is that you can publish your work that you may or may not do inside the classroom. But you can publish it to other people and get feedback on it. That's where it's getting really exciting. When they understand they are not producing for a teacher to receive a mark, but they are producing in order to communicate. (HS, French Teacher)

I didn't really understand what they (i.e. digital stories) were at all before we started, but now that I've made one I can see how much easier it is. And it's just another good way to communicate with people. (HS M.)

In time digital communication—and putting together the kind of things that we've done, and the way we can do it, and the way we communicate, and the way we narrate, and the way that move around, and find out information—but also get a feeling of what this history of Aboriginal Sydney's being all about. What kind of

(Continued)

(cont'd)

feeling do I get from it, which you get easier from a film and from a book, and from a novel or non-fiction? How is that going to emerge? I think it should emerge, I am sure it will eventually, but that's something I don't quite understand and that's probably something we'll all develop in the future. (HoAS, Peter Read)

The possibility of presenting multisensory information in new ways introduces the possibility of including content that has not been part of traditional academic output. These new possibilities could hardly be understood and appreciated theoretically, as they are based on experience and hands-on practice as much as on intellectual understanding. For Peter Read, experience of presenting academic research online brought a realization that digital media open possibilities of qualitatively new genres:

We know what film can do and what it can't do, but we are still exploring the boundaries. It takes a long long time to understand that. And we don't have any idea ...not where we will go, but where we can go. And it's really exciting to think about it, and emotional intelligence is one really exciting part. And it shouldn't be just communicated in videos either. How it's communicated in other ways, I really've got no idea, but that's a really exciting field, which other people besides me will have to carry forward... We have to think of it as a new form of communication, just like radio, just like books, novels, non-fiction, movies... Not just a way of communication. Well, they are, there is always communication, but something more specific and more stand-alone, as I realise it now, than I actually understood in the beginning. Not just like an encyclopedia and it's not just like an index.

3.4.2 Learning

[It] helps me, [with] what I'm imagining just to put it visually and show others without me having to explain it. So I could just think of a story, make a comic, do a digital story.

HS B.

Abundant data about various forms of learning were gathered during the project. Adults in the study reflected on their developing knowledge and skills as a result of transliterate ways of working, while their academic outputs provided some observable evidence and examples of their comments. For the monitoring of teenagers' learning, there were some distinct advantages of data-gathering in a school where I worked. Student observation, teachers' comments, school records are all within reach to contribute to a fuller understanding of learning processes. Based on insights from participants' self-assessment and teachers' evaluation over a period of several years, it can be said with confidence that transliterate ways of working can provide some unique formal and informal learning opportunities.

3.4.2.1   Overall learning outcomes

High school students were consistently asked during the study to comment on their learning. Initial data-gathering was through surveys at the end of a project when students had opportunities to assess their learning individually while providing first rounds of data for further exploration in interviews and focus groups. Many of their observations were shared in this chapter, but survey data provide another way of looking into student perception of their learning.

Students were asked to rate statements about their learning in transliteracy projects by using a four point Likert scale (i.e., strongly disagree to strongly agree). Fig. 3.7 shows how students in iTell assessed various aspects of their learning in digital storytelling workshops, indicating very positive perceptions. Similar assessments were proffered by students in the game coding program LevelUp. All students in LevelUp agreed or strongly agreed with the statement "I feel more confident about using coding." Of 16 students in the Enrichment program who completed the survey, 2 disagreed and 14 agreed or strongly agreed with the statement "I learnt a lot about truth and reality." In the French class, all except one agreed or strongly agreed with the statements "I learnt a lot about French school life" and "My French has improved." Altogether, 55 students responded to survey questions about their learning in transliteracy projects indicating a high level of satisfaction with their learning—statements attracted an average rating of at least 3 out of 4 (Table 3.2).

All educators, librarians, and teachers involved in the projects made very positive assessments of the process of learning and student results. The French class provides a useful example, as this transliteracy project was conducted under regular classroom conditions and included a formal assessment. The teacher and the physical setting were not changed for the French transliteracy project. School life has been used as the topic for several years with Year 10 French classes providing opportunities to monitor changes introduced with the transliteracy project as compared with results in the previous years. The French teacher involved in the

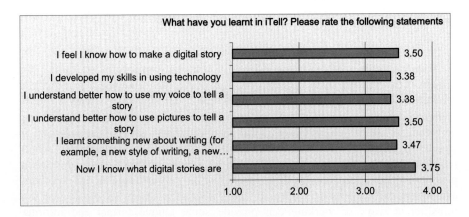

Figure 3.7 iTell survey. Student perception of learning.

Table 3.2 Student self-assessment of their learning

Project	Statement	Student self-assessment of their learning (max. value #4)
iTell	6 statements in Fig. 3.7	3.49 average
LevelUp	I feel more confident about using code	3.4
Enrichment	I learnt a lot about truth & reality	3.06
French	I learnt a lot about French	3.15
	My French has improved	3.15
Total no. of responses: 55		

transliteracy project taught this topic at the college in the previous years. As outlined in Chapter 2, *Study of Transliteracy: Approach*, some aspects of teaching in the French class were changed to incorporate transliteracy.

In previous years, students were assessed in oral examinations, while in the transliteracy project, students were assessed on videos of their French conversations with other students. The preparation of videos was an integral part of their learning. The teacher found that the quality of student recorded conversations in French was better than the students had traditionally demonstrated in oral exams. "Something must have worked—whether it was the association with the image (or) writing it a few times until copy was correct," she said. The teacher was very pleased with the level of grammar students had demonstrated. Students, on the other hand, enjoyed what they perceived as less explicit teaching of grammar, although this was not the case according to the teacher. She said that students learned relevant grammar early in the program and had more opportunities to use it and understand it better. A realistic conversational situation also led to a more natural use of the language. The teacher thought that the screening of videos was a powerful motivation for girls to present their best attempt: "Everyone says it's such a beautiful language, and to hear yourself and see yourself performing in that language—it's just another level of keeping their motivation up." Students commented on their improved confidence in speaking French when they realized they were understood by other students.

Considering that the students prepared their recorded conversations, there was a possibility that their language skills could not be replicated in less predictable oral exams. The teacher, however, did not think that was the case and explained: "If I said, here are some sample questions, six of these questions will come up in your exam, I am convinced that some girls would have had one sentence or nothing to say for certain questions. Whereas if you watch videos, they are all decent answers." Another opportunity to test gains in student learning presented itself several months later when students sat for their yearly examinations and achieved very high results. The teacher commented that this particular group consisted of many motivated students, but their results were better than expected. "We went from transliteracy project into Term 4 and into preparation for the exam. I was lucky they were already on the high and they maintained that. I think if we've done something completely different in Term 3, it'd be harder getting them up to that level."

3.4.2.2   Learning across

Examples from the French project provide a sense of the type of learning in which peers, creativity, technology, and personal interests may come together to enhance learning and make potentially difficult aspects more palatable. Insights into the development of digital, writing, social, and communication skills provide a perspective on "learning across" showing how transliteracy fosters nonlinear and unintentional learning.

Digital skills were an important part of learning in transliteracy projects, although not always central to it. For many students, using technology in a creative way and learning through doing for a particular purpose were rewarding aspects of the transliteracy work. In the technology-rich environment, students observed how they acquired skills they did not initially have in mind, such as file conversion or image manipulation techniques.

Digital citizenship and knowledge about copyright had become a particularly interesting aspect of learning, as students either spent hours looking for suitable music and images for their digital stories or decided to ignore the rules and were consequently unable to publish their work. Student N. commented on the frustration and her learning in the process of collecting resources online, from searching techniques and the organization of her own work, and then reflected on copyright issues: "I think it was nice to finally look at how much you take off the internet that is actually copyrighted so, if you really think about it, you don't have much that is copyright free or stuff that people will make copyright free. So, yeah, that was quite nice." Another junior student commented that learning about copyright was a particularly interesting aspect of iTell, hardly a comment one would expect to hear from a high school student. In one of the workshops, a concern was raised about the use of a short clip from a commercial film. A junior student who wanted to use the clip readily responded with information about the permitted use of film excerpts, demonstrating not only the awareness of the issue, but also that she obtained the correct information about permitted use.

Writing. The digital storytelling workshops provided ample opportunities for exploring new writing approaches and techniques. A talented young writer discussed in some detail how iTell opened "a new type of writing" for her. This new type of writing is to do with the economy of expression and multimodality, and also the involvement of other students and thinking about collaboration in writing. Another student commented:

> I sort of I learned... the different ways of writing... like writing from the objects' point of view and things like that. But just ...writing in a group, like having other people's opinions to write stories cos I don't really really talk to people about the stuff I write. So just having that other persons' perspective on what I was writing was very good.
>
> *HS H.*

Student T. observed she had never thought she could write effectively a story of about 200 words, but images helped her: "I think the pictures probably helped us to write more. Little details in the pictures, you can expand on them. And that images give you, tell you the story themselves" (HS T.). Academics commented in the same vein on learning from online interactions to write differently. A scholar discussed essentially the same idea as student T. when she commented on how she explored fonts and visual elements to communicate on the page.

A multiplicity of voices has prominent place in writing explorations. A large group of iTell students modeled collaborative writing and representation of different tones and voices as they assembled a digital story consisting of different perspectives and sources. It is, essentially, a similar process to what an academic described in this way: "Often in academic writing I write with this persuasive single voice, but I also think there're ways to write where . . .on any one, say, run of five pages, you might have three different styles or different voices. . . So all of them making the text so that you get this interweave of different registers or modes or moods" (U Participant 6/2).

"Learning across" provides opportunities for learners of any age to discover interests and acquire new skills. Academics with very little interest in technology described how they embarked on some substantial digital projects once they decided to use technology to complete a task which could not be easily completed in other ways. A number of students noted how they enjoyed doing something and felt proud of the results, although they had initially thought they lacked aptitude and interest. Students who struggled with writing, for example, made a start by combining visual storyboards, notes on a mind map and oral storytelling to gradually develop a piece of writing. This way of working resembles an extended power board on which different power points can be used to "plug in." In a similar way, a student can develop multiskilling and the ability to work in different modalities by engaging through the one point where they feel most comfortable.

Social skills, communication, and confidence. The development of confidence, social skills, and ways of dealing with personal and social issues has been noted as a very significant aspect of school transliteracy workshops. This was especially the case when workshops were organized as whole day immersion opportunities or in a special interest group such as LevelUp. Opportunities to connect gently and through a channel that inspires self-confidence create a setting for exploration. Rules for interactions were normally established early in the program, providing a framework and a safe environment for engagement and exploration. For many girls, it was the right environment in which to reflect on personal issues and concerns, such as bullying, through an intimate, but still impersonal story. Many girls commented on their growing confidence, as a result of participating in iTell, in particular. With some self-assurance, a sense of trust, and a guiding framework for behavior, students learned valuable social skills, which was sometimes noted by teachers outside workshops.

All transliteracy projects had a presentation component when work results were shared with an audience. Presentations for the school community, participation in competitions, publishing work on the website and in a youth electronic publication brought another dimension to school work. In many instances, decisions about presentation were not made in advance, developing with student confidence and interests. For students who were reluctant to present their work, examples of positive feedback and meaningful engagement with the audience inspired confidence and encouraged them to try it next time or regret that they had not finished their work in time to participate. For a group of students who expressed low self-esteem in relation to their school work on many occasions in the iTell workshops and during data-gathering, feedback from the College community after public screening had a more powerful impact than anything an individual educator could have said. It could be observed by subtle demonstrations of pride in student body language, willingness to participate in subsequent related events and own initiatives to apply skills learned in digital storytelling workshops elsewhere. In all these cases, opportunities to move across the learning fields in a structured and organized, but flexible manner, allowed intentional and unintentional learning to occur on different levels.

3.4.2.3 Are these lasting results?

It is difficult, if not impossible, to tease out various influences on the formation of students, although results of learning in transliteracy projects could be followed to an extent outside immediate outcomes. It was particularly the case with iTell because it was the first transliteracy project with opportunities for diverse data-gathering over a longer period of time. iTell also benefited from consistent use of teaching methods and techniques congruent with transliteracy—a project-based and student-centered learning in a physical setting and time-frame conducive to engagement.

iTell students demonstrated retention of skills and maintained interest and motivation in a way that could be related to their experience with transliteracy. They were able to apply digital storytelling skills if they participated in subsequent digital storytelling workshops or decided to make digital stories for other purposes. French students, as mentioned above, retained the learning focus and mastering of grammar a few months after the project. The majority of junior students who became involved with transliteracy workshops and projects in 2012 and 2013 remained involved in a range of similar events and initiatives provided by the library. The fact that they remained interested in transliterate experiences is a testament of their engagement with these types of activity, although personal inclinations may have played a part.

It is likely that students who participated in iTell and benefited from similar opportunities during junior years have developed some distinct skills and insights. One of the students used her skills in visual storytelling for the major work required for the matriculation examination in Design and Technology (Higher School Certificate in New South Wales, Australia). A teacher who prepared some of the former iTell students for their major matriculation examination in Drama noted that these girls excelled in their ability to communicate theoretical understanding in other forms. The teacher commented that many Drama students are good at either practical work or understanding complex texts, but very few have an ability to do both very well and, especially, to connect insights from the two domains. The

Drama teacher, however, thought that the whole group was evidently different from the majority of students in their ability to move across theoretical, performative, and technical aspects of Drama.

Students often commented on how iTell helped them to develop their creativity. Student B., one of the students whose abilities were discussed by the Drama teacher, made the following comment about becoming more creative after iTell at the time when she was a junior student:

> B: Yeah I've been doing some of the stuff that I ... wouldn't normally do, like digital storytelling, as I said—I've been doing some of that. And some of the other stuff we've been doing in classes, like getting more creative because of some of the things I've learnt.
> SS: So how are you ... being more creative? What have you done?
> B: Well in one of my classes we were learning how to make some Christmas decorations, so I've been doing some of those, and the digital storytelling ...
> SS: How does storytelling help you with decorations?
> B: Well it makes ... helps me what I'm imagining, just to put it visually and show others without me having to explain it. So I could just think of a story, make a comic, do a digital story.

For some students, outcomes were noted in temporary or apparently lasting shifts in attitudes and behaviors. Particularly prominent is an example of student J. who joined iTell on the recommendation of her Year Advisor as a creative, but consistently disengaged student. This student participated in two rounds of iTell in a year, worked well, and discussed her delight with the experience. Fig. 3.8 shows her response to the "one-minute paper" before iTell in which she notes her hopes that she would not be bored, which she thought was "most unlikely," and that she would not be told how to write her own stories. This response is accompanied by her enthusiastic evaluation of her experience in iTell. A change of J.'s attitude toward learning was observed by teachers immediately after iTell. Her report at the end of the year noted a significant improvement in academic results and attitude. In the following year, J. was included in the Enrichment program for gifted and talented students. In subsequent years, J. excelled in areas of her interest and remained engaged in library activities, which required critical thinking, collaboration, and creativity.

It is very difficult to tease out various short- and long-term influences on learning with confidence, and this is particularly the case with short-term programs. However, prolonged data-gathering strengthened the case for the benefits of transliterate approaches to learning representing a rich area for investigation.

3.4.2.4 Is transliterate learning different from learning in a regular classroom?

I asked this question in the first round of iTell interviews as a way of discerning some difference, if any, between workshop and classroom experiences. I believed that students already had similar learning opportunities in class and did not expect a straightforward "yes, very different." Surprised by the same answer from all iTell

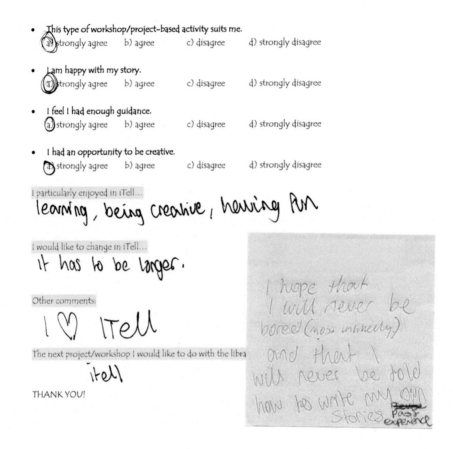

Figure 3.8 Student J's response before and after iTell.

students who answered in the initial round, I included this question in subsequent data-gathering and, overall, confirmed the initial student response.

Answers from Enrichment and French classes were particularly relevant as transliteracy projects were developed within the regular classroom schedule with the same teacher. Enrichment classes had some whole day workshops, which was not the regular school practice, but French classes worked exactly as they had done before with regular periods and, as mentioned earlier, the same teacher and final assessment. As Table 3.3 shows, most students in Enrichment classes found that their experiences in the transliteracy project were different from both their regular classes and other Enrichment lessons. All French students said the transliteracy project was different. The French students explained points of difference in the focus group, mentioning the use of technology, interactivity, practical independent work, script writing and opportunities to practice speaking more than grammar while preparing videos. Responses of the Enrichment students indicated project-based learning, deep investigation of personal interests, opportunities for immersion

Table 3.3 Answers to survey questions about similarity with regular classroom experience

Question	#Agree & Strongly Agree/ #Survey responses
Enrichment classes this semester were very different from what we normally do in regular classes	14/16
Enrichment classes this semester were very different from what we normally do in Enrichment	13/16
French classes this term were very different from what we normally do in French	13/13

and research during whole days in the library, and creative approaches to presentation of their results in the final expo.

The comparison with regular classes raises more questions than it answers. "Which classroom?," "What sort of learning?" are we comparing? How indicative are experiences at the college of other learning environments? On one hand, the study data are too limited to provide answers with confidence. On the other, definitive answers are not possible because there are always too many variants and transliteracy is contextually bound by definition. However, we can have a glimpse by looking through the lens of data gathered in this study. That glimpse is telling us that transliteracy can make a qualitative difference in student learning.

Some differences between iTell and regular classes:

N: First of all, the skills that we learned like the technology skills. Those were really good because even though we do need to use them a lot more in class, we don't really get a lot of time to learn about it and teachers often don't really know a lot about it either. Then also, I think, being able to talk to other people and get other ideas from people because a lot of the time I find that I just work by myself. If I'm not sure, I try to work it out by myself. I often don't ask questions and ask other people.
SS: Does this encourage you to ask more questions?
N: Yeah, I think so.
SS: In what way?
N: Just because it's more of a group atmosphere and the story circle and things like that where we sat around and talked about things, it felt like a really productive exercise. [HS Student M. about iTell]

SS: Do you think it's a different way of working than in the class apart from the length?
N: Yes. Cos it's very different in the number of teachers and the age gap of the girls and also how we never really look at...It's hard to explain, but you don't in school hours... they have exams you have to work for. But in iTell you're only

(Continued)

(cont'd)

really working for that digital story. It's nothing quite pressuring about it except that you have to get it done. But, yeah, it's different and it's not because you still have the goal. But how it's treated with the activities and the people who are invited in and, yeah, I would say that it's very different. (HS N.)

iTell is very different from other classes—less instruction, lot more creative space, lot more fun. (HS C.)

A different style of learning as perceived by a student in an Enrichment class:

It was also a different learning style and that really developed what we learned as well. If we are in a normal class, it's all, copy down what's on the whiteboard, or make notes from this [book work—another voice] every single lesson. It was good to have a different style of learning because it exposes us to different ways of finding out the research that we needed. (HS, Enrichment)

How does transliteracy contribute to learning and knowledge production? Summary

• New perspectives, insights, and approaches are enabled through multisensory and multimodal practices, different tones and voices, and new means of communication of knowledge.
• Enhanced learning of skills and content.
• "Learning across" occurs as students connect different skills and domains.
• Indications of medium- to long-term effects on learning among school students.

3.5 Summary

The conceptual model of transliteracy was introduced in this chapter. Results from the study on transliteracy were considered in relation to the research questions.

1. The main aspects which constitute transliteracy are interactions with a multiplicity of resources with different qualities, and working with materials by using a range of media technologies and techniques. These types of interaction open new lines of investigation and creative approaches and often involve sense-making by connecting disparate information and ideas. Working with others by communicating and collaborating in person and via digital media, across social groupings, is an important aspect of transliteracy. Netchaining, as a practice of establishing and shaping information chains which link sources and people, is part of the process of information searching and networking. Results of transliterate ways of working are communicated by incorporating different tones, voices, modalities, and genres.

2. Transliteracy is predominantly experienced as an engaging, exploratory, and creative way of working. A sense of connection with others and establishing one's "own voice" is an important part of the experience. In some instances, frustration and anxiety are associated with information overload, working with technology and interactions with others.
3. Transliteracy contributes to learning and knowledge production by enabling new perspectives, insights and approaches through multisensory and multimodal practices, different tones and voices, and new methods of communication of knowledge. "Learning across" occurs as learners connect different skills and domains. Learning of skills and the content is enhanced, as indicated by student perception (as reported in feedback) and teachers' assessment and observation. Transliteracy in learning and knowledge production is a promising area for further investigation.

The definition of transliteracy from the beginning of this chapter arises from the analysis of the research data.

References

ACARA, 2013. General capabilities. Australian Curriculum, Assessment and Reporting Authority. Available from: http://www.acara.edu.au/curriculum (accessed 24.04.16.).

Al-Shboul, M.K., Abrizah, A., 2014. Information needs: developing personas of humanities scholars. J. Acad. Librar. 40, 500–509.

Dalton, M.S., Charnigo, L., 2004. Historians and their information sources. College Res. Librar. 65, 400–425.

Houghton, J.W., Steele, C., Henty, M., 2003. Changing research practices in the digital information and communication environment. Department of Education, Science and Training, Canberra.

Latour, B., 2005. Reassembling the Social: an Introduction to Actor-Network-Theory. Clarendon, Oxford.

Palmer, C.L., 2005. Scholarly work and the shaping of digital access. J. Am. Soc. Inform. Sci. Technol. 56, 1140–1153.

Palmer, C.L., Neumann, L.J., 2002. The information work of interdisciplinary humanities scholars: exploration and translation. Librar. Quarter. 72, 85–117.

Read, P., 15 June 2016. RE: Research 30 years ago and now. Type to SUKOVIC, S.

RULOIS, 2002. See Education for Change Ltd.

Sukovic, S., 2008. Convergent flows: humanities scholars and their interactions with electronic texts. Librar. Quarter. 78, 263–284.

Sukovic, S., 2011. E-texts in research projects in the humanities. In: Woodsworth, A. (Ed.), Advances in Librarianship, Vol. 33. Emerald Group Publishing Limited, Bingley.

Sze, G.S., Ngah, Z.A., 1997. Postgraduate research in the humanities at the University of Malaya. Malaysian J. Librar. Inform. Sci. 2, 71–80.

Wiberley, S.E., Jones, W.G., 1989. Patterns of information seeking in the humanities. College Res. Librar.638–645.

Transliteracy in practice

4

After exploring the meanings and instances of transliteracy in Chapter 3, Exploring Transliteracy, the next question is what it all means in practice. The chapter starts by considering the last research question concerning aids and challenges to transliteracy. The rest of the chapter is devoted to different aspects of transliteracy in formal and informal learning. Transliteracy and learning, pedagogies for transliteracy, and the blurring line between reader, user, and creator are considered in some detail, providing a solid ground for evidence-based practice.

4.1 Aids and challenges

The last research question in the study of transliteracy concerns aids and challenges for transliterate ways of learning and knowledge production. Key aids and challenges are grouped around two issues:

- Underpinning structures—technology, access to information, and work time and space
- Transliteracy capabilities—particularly in relation to skills and traditions, professional development, and collaboration. A need for support expressed by participants is also considered.

4.1.1 Structures: IT, information access, time and space

And because cultural studies are eclectic, trying to break the mould, you just see in . . . catalogues and everything just that reproduction of those sort of hierarchies and disciplinarity which we're trying to break down. And it was always a fantasy that electronics and digitalisation would help break those down. . .

Participant 7/1

All aids and challenges are in some way related to information infrastructures. Particularly prominent are those which define tools and access to information as they are major enablers, and also the most difficult to change on a local level. Time and space for transliteracy projects are determined locally and, by their nature, outline the context in which projects can unfold.

4.1.1.1 Information technology

Solid computers with useful and appropriate software, connected to a robust network, are necessary for most types of work nowadays, and especially for transliteracy work. Software for collaborative ways of working and sharing is very important, but according to study participants, it is very often either unavailable or not functioning properly. Academics in particular require user-friendly software for

Transliteracy in Complex Information Environments. DOI: http://dx.doi.org/10.1016/B978-0-08-100875-1.00004-2

certain tasks, but there is often a gap between what is needed and what is available. For example, at the time when interviews were conducted, they struggled with software for manipulating large digital maps or for voice recognition and transcription.

While new technologies often trigger new ways of working, many participants of all ages believed that old and new technology have some unique advantages. Digital technology is not perceived as reliable by some so it should not replace analog technologies. Participant 7/1 commented, "Well, also there's … still the underlying fear that if it's electronic, it can be wiped. Entirely." This researcher kept everything in hard copy if it was possible.

Attitudes to working with technology could be a major enabler or a stumbling block. It was particularly evident with students who either claimed they were not "good with technology" or, in one case, preferred not to use any of the online tools. All academics who demonstrated elaborate transliterate behaviors were open to using any technology that was likely to enable effective work. Although attitudes to technology may be a result of experience, they are also likely to have some impact on practices.

4.1.1.2 Access to information

Access to information is another well-established contemporary requirement. While students usually discussed the value of having access to well-organized information of good quality in the library, academics commented on information structures and politics of access, which often impose restrictions. The conditions of database use and organizational access impose artificial boundaries around information. Information provision was described as a reproduction of societal hierarchies. Participant 7/1 commented:

> *Everything either belongs to a journal, a particular journal, or a particular kind of academic field. So, ideally, I'd like to be able to search for Cook across academic articles that have been published in all fields, you know, but you just can't do it. So it takes ages. And because cultural studies are eclectic, trying to break the mould, you just see in … catalogues and everything just that reproduction of those sort of hierarchies and disciplinarity which we're trying to break down. And it was always a fantasy that electronics and digitalisation would help break those down, but where you've broken down a kind of a discipline or a field category, then what's intervened is the power of a publishing corporation.*

Limited rights, and issues of technical and intellectual access were noted as barriers in using sophisticated technology. As mentioned in previous sections, students also commented on copyright and branding restrictions. For them, it was not only a matter of frustration about finding copyright-free resources but also a reflection on the protection of online resources. Participant 15/1 and his team decided not to use some innovative applications as they would limit access to the content.

Availability of digital information is an issue in some fields. Alongside the abundance of information that has been made available with or without restrictions, there is a "poverty of knowledge about many areas of the globe," Participant 14/1 commented and added:

> *I happen to work in American history and if I want to look up anything about American history, I can find it out very easily on the net. And I think that encourages more knowledge about America. But, you know, I've just been looking up, because of the work that I'm doing, the work of Martin Delaney and other people in Africa and if I want to go back and I want to find out how the colony of Liberia was established and how Sierra Leone developed as freed slaves, etc., I'm much better off going back to books. There's a poverty of knowledge about many areas of the globe.*

4.1.1.3 Time and space

Time and space which allows uninterrupted work and a sense of immersion was greatly appreciated by students and academics alike. Most academics discussed organization of work around inevitable interruptions in their offices so they would do tasks such as searching at work, and reading and writing at home or sometimes in the library. Students greatly appreciated whole day workshops when they could feel immersed in their work. Many commented on how they had time to think during these days and complete most substantial parts of their work.

Comfortable space where one can relax and devote attention to work was important. Some academics talked about libraries and archives as places of knowledge, which they enjoyed. Many students commented on how they liked being in the library as it was a pleasant and comfortable environment, which affected how they learned: "Helps you to think in a relaxing way, because we don't do lessons in the library. In the classroom we would experience it differently," an Enrichment student commented. For iTell students, free use of space was a very important aspect of their experience. They worked lying on couches, sitting on the floor, or under the tables, choosing the right proximity to the rest of the group. Flexible use of space also signaled a different and more creative learning environment. Thomas (2013) noted Pullinger's observation that space for transliteracy should be interdisciplinary and it should encourage interaction as well as individual work. Whole day sessions when students had time and space to spread out, be comfortable, and feel immersed in the content of their work were conducive to learning.

4.1.2 Skill development

> **We can start teaching new media writers, artists, theorists etc., a kind of critical media literacy that engages them in such a way that they learn to improve various stages of development so that they can become... better performers of writing.**
>
> *Participant 15/1*

The development of transliteracy skills is essential, but a very difficult task as it requires much more than organizing courses and workshops. Some indications of aids, issues, and possible solutions are arising from the study data.

4.1.2.1   Traditions and skills

The acceptance and promotion of transliteracy depend to a large extent on academic traditions, discipline, and transliteracy skills. A critical issue is that traditional ways of working in research and educational institutions limit developing transliteracy. Educational institutions favor traditional outputs because they suit established forms of performance evaluation and institutional rankings. High school students are usually assessed on the basis of formal examinations, essays, reports, oral presentations, and discipline-specific outputs. Academics are assessed mainly on the basis of their peer-reviewed papers and books. Other forms of output, especially those crossing disciplinary boundaries, are difficult to assess, and hence are accepted as perhaps valuable and discretionary but not as core activities. This point was reiterated in many conversations with academic study participants. Some senior academics pointed out they were more likely to experiment because formal evaluations had little impact on their careers.

The link between academia and the profession aiming to enable a strong connection between theory and practice is often publicly promoted, but not supported in reality. Professional experience is regarded as counting very little in academic promotions in many institutions, as Participant 2/2 discussed in relation to an applied academic field:

SS: Do you think that if you could use something like audio to support your research, your academic output, do you think that this is accepted and valued?

Participant 2/2: There is huge lobbying and all kinds of things to get it valued. It should be, I think, incorporated into the point system, and the professional practice. I know there are people here at [university] who applied for scholarships and things who haven't been able to get their work counted as research output even though it's hugely valued in terms of their employment. So they are employed here because of that, but when it comes to research side of things that's not counted at all.

Academic traditions and skill acquisition work together in a vicious circle. A historian commented on how difficult it is to assess collaborative and electronic work when the emphasis of academic evaluation is clearly on individual contribution and traditional output. Because it pays off to write academic publications, academics are less inclined to learn and use other skills. But, because the skill base is lacking, it is more difficult to promote transliterate ways of working. Academics commented on the absence of adequate education and training to prepare them for transliterate knowledge production. They also suggested what could be done to change this situation (see examples in outlined quotes). The complexity of change is compounded by the fact that university students are already primed to work in traditional ways. Although there are some notable exceptions, high schools are often focused on preparing students for traditional academic success, especially as measured by external examinations. As mentioned in the previous section in relation to contributions to learning, high school students in the study commented on how different transliterate ways of working were from their regular classroom experiences. Part of that difference is related to collaborative learning, creativity, the use of different technologies, and a shift to presenting output as a form of communication rather than for external assessment. Another part is to do with time and space for exploration and immersion. One of the Enrichment students commented: "I need a project to work on. If it's going to class every lesson and it's—having something to work on, you are building on it. And every lesson you feel fulfilled."

> *I don't think that anything is done to promote the use of electronic media. Where this shows up is in teaching. There's not a single course that we teach in this department in which there is, which is devoted to history students or history graduate students learning about the use of electronic sources. (U Participant 14/1)*
> *But I think people don't actually know what's out there so I think there could be a lot more projects and we could have PhD students working or we could have more of a team based approach to things. But I think people are doing what they are doing. And a lot of people I worked with in radio are not actually in the radio history or media history. Only other person I know who does what I am doing is someone who went to UTS so he has this theory-practice crossover so I think that's the unique media studies-cultural studies approach, which comes from a degree when you've done production and you understand production side of things. (U Participant 2/2)*
> *And digital communication—that's an important one, and if it's possible to introduce students to digital communication in the way of creating it, not just using it, of course, but a way of creating it, that would be a pretty valuable step forward. In other words, you say to people, to your students, 'You're going to do an interview with somebody—good. A. take a video camera. B. don't just send them [i.e. interviewees] a video back. What are you going to do with this material? How are you going to use to communicate to the family and to other people as well? Let's think about the ways of disseminating this information'. Now, it's only the very first step. It's not what we were talking about just now in terms of videos, I mean, the websites being a different form of communication. But nevertheless it's a step forward towards that. (HoAS Peter Read)*
> *This is something that I think we can do in an educational context because we can start teaching new media writers, artists, theorists etc., a kind of critical media literacy that engages them in such a way that they learn to improve various stages of development [so] that they can become, I don't know, better performers [you might say], better performers of writing. (U Participant 15/1)*

4.1.2.2 Professional development

Professional development of teachers on all levels is critically important to support students in developing new skills and exploring transliterate ways of working. However, both academics and high school teachers discussed limitations in their preparedness. When Participant 14/1 explained how students do not learn about electronic tools and resources, I asked whether academics need to learn about it as well:

> *Yeah. Undoubtedly. There is no in-service kind of training, there's no seminars, I've never heard of a staff seminar about this. . . It's something that might be discussed in the staffroom as a kind of lunchtime topic, along with plagiarism and whatever else but . . . Historians are not terribly reflexive about their own practice. So they're all just using it kind of willy-nilly, everybody learns, no-one ever told me to use them, no-one ever gave me any instruction at all. And that's probably reflected in my serendipitous way of going about it. And my ignorance of certain things. **It's kind of like a benign neglect.***
>
> U Participant 14/1, emphasis by SS

An academic from another institution commented in a similar vein that there was no discussion about electronic media and resources and no one who could provide advice. A senior academic commented on the conundrum of professional learning when timing and purpose are as important as the provision of learning opportunities:

> *If you're not sufficiently trained or taught how to use it [i.e. technology and search tools] efficiently, you can waste an awful lot of time being incompetent, as I suspect is the case with me. But in order to be trained and taught properly, you have to take time out from other things and so you tend not to do it. You think, well, I will learn how to do this if I'm learning how to do it in doing my own research. You tend to remember things if they're important to you. Whereas if somebody is just saying, 'Well, here's a program, you can do x, y and z with it and you can do this and this' . . . Unless I want to do any of those things, I just forget it, it just means nothing to me. I think with a much younger generation of people who grow up with computers automatically, this will not be a problem. But for people like me, there's neither the appropriate training to exploit these things properly or else we resist it because we think there are other things to do.*
>
> U Participant 6/1

In the high school environment, highly motivated teachers discussed similar inadequacies in preparing educators for innovative teaching. A common complaint is that the only time to promote new practices is in staff meetings and in-service opportunities when teachers are being given information with limited or no time to discuss new ideas and innovative teaching approaches. The French teacher commented on the excited response of the Languages Department when they were invited to contribute to transliteracy curriculum mapping. "It's all about hands on, the concrete," she said.

4.1.2.3 Collaboration

Collaboration is being considered in this section as an aid for transliterate practices. Learning in collaboration with peers has already been discussed, but it is worth pointing out some of the ways in which collaboration supports transliterate forms of learning.

For the French students, it was valuable to have plenty of opportunity to hear differences in how people speak the language. It was not just the teacher who was asking questions but also student peers, so changes of roles and practicing both questions and answers supported learning. With adults' help, students can be more effective in encouraging each other to persevere. Student B. commented about her experience in iTell:

> They [i.e. other students] gave me a lot of ideas and advice on how it should be written or they told me what their story was about so I go, 'Oh, maybe I should write that'. They help me to write in a different way and it was also fun listening to their stories as well. I mean if I was all by myself I don't think I would be able to do it as easily. I would be stuck. Still.

Unlike set group work, collaborative work in transliteracy projects was to a large extent voluntary. In digital storytelling projects, students chose how much they wanted to be involved with others. Student Y. liked working close to others while maintaining a sense of separation: "That gave us almost some room to breathe or something."

For academics, communication and collaboration arising from transliterate practices were very beneficial. Formal collaboration is becoming more prominent in the humanities, one participant observed. She attributed it to a better understanding of how research breakthroughs are achieved, an active push from an Australian key funding body, and a more prominent presence of women in research. The result is that "the problems are more complex as well, looking across national contexts or geographical contexts because there are many interesting work that comes out because people are coming together and being engaged across different distances" (U Participant 2/2).

Collaboration requires a wide range of skills, from technical, project management, understanding of protocols and ethics to an organizational culture of collaboration, and reflection embedded in the professional practice. It is hardly surprising that sustained collaboration is rarely a common practice in schools and university humanities departments. Skills in collaboration do not come naturally to generations who did not learn how to collaborate at school and who do not work in teams on a regular basis. Although collaboration appears as an easy-to-adopt soft skill, the reality is very different. Many teachers and academics, who are used to working on their own and with students, need much more than an opportunity to work collaboratively to develop new skills and practices.

4.1.2.4   Assistance and support

While formal learning in the classroom and professional development opportunities are needed, assistance and guidance at the time of need are highly valued by students, teachers, and academics. Many of them need someone who knows sources and understands the content to guide them through the process.

High school students appreciated individual explorations supported by guidance and scaffolding. Students in iTell often commented on their appreciation of the knowledgeable guidance library staff had offered in digital storytelling workshops. Students in the Enrichment classes liked scaffolding provided by resources as well as feedback from their teacher and librarian. One of the students commented on the benefits of working in the library with staff "who were interested in that topic and who knew about it because they learnt about it before. And we had any book that we wanted to read, and any resources that we needed we can access easily, so that really helped." Another student commented on a helpful combination of advice and resources while her peers confirmed her comments: "I looked at all those books that you suggested to me—because I wasn't sure before that. Once I started reading through, it gave me ideas of topics. And it was more detailed and I trusted it more than using the Internet."

In a similar way, the French teacher commented on how it was helpful to implement transliteracy in existing programs. She suggested that many professional learning initiatives could be taken by following the flipped classroom model where teachers would have a chance to hear an introduction, reflect on what they are already doing, and then work with a specialist on implementation. "If it sits on that abstract level, it will always be in a 'too hard' basket," this teacher commented.

Academics expressed a need to have the assistance of a highly specialized information professional who had a good knowledge not only of the subject area but also of a narrow field. Researchers who explored very broad topics felt overwhelmed and wished to have someone on call who could help them. Knowledge of scholarly protocols and a comprehensive understanding of databases were also required.

What are some aids and challenges? Summary
- Reliable networks and computers; software that can support particular tasks
- Access to information across domains and subject fields
- Time for immersion and space that can be used freely
- Need for teaching and learning transliteracy skills
- Limitations imposed by some educational and academic traditions
- Comprehensive support for professional development
- Benefits of collaboration and need for skill development
- Guidance and practical support by knowledgeable professionals needed.

4.2 Transliteracy and learning

Transliteracy belongs in the information and knowledge field in a broad sense, so it is hardly surprising that the crux of discussions about aids and challenges revolves around capabilities and learning. The rest of this chapter will be devoted to considerations of what transliteracy means for the practices of teaching and learning.

Transliteracy is a powerful epistemic framework, grounded in experience, easily related to thinking about information practice in the modern world. Its broad meaning also leaves an impression that transliteracy is difficult to grasp. We may agree it is important, but can it be taught? Where do we start with it? Transliteracy assumes a skill set, and also a range of meanings and behaviors with complex underpinnings. It has connections with conceptual thinking, but it is firmly grounded in practice. Transliteracy is about a combination of knowledge and competencies that enables a person to work and live in complex information environments. These environments are changeable and their contexts are many and different. New technologies appear almost daily and educators have difficulties keeping up with all of them. In order to be useful, transliteracy needs to be understood as a dynamic, flexible, yet applicable framework in different educational contexts.

4.2.1 Transliteracy palettes

A model of transliteracy palettes is proposed as a tool to aid the development of transliteracy in teaching and learning. Transliteracy palettes are based on the conceptual understanding presented in Fig 3.1. They emerged as a result of iterations of inductive and deductive approaches in thinking how a broad concept can be applied in the practice of teaching and learning. They are based on reading, experience, and conversations with colleagues in the education and information professions and, importantly, are grounded in the research data.

Transliteracy palettes describe what people have at their disposal to shape their transliterate practice and understanding. Transliteracy palettes consist of an *information palette* and a *form palette*.

Information palette (Fig. 4.1). Information and ICT capabilities have already been identified as critical to one aspect of transliteracy. These capabilities are also integrated in the well-established information literacy framework. The components of the information palette are closely aligned with the ACRL information literacy framework and standards (ACRL, 2000, 2016) and the Australia and New Zealand information literacy framework (Bundy, 2004), which have become a key part of library and information, as well as educational, practice (The New South Wales Department of Education and Training, 2007; Hobbs, 2011). The understanding of the information process presented in the information palette draws upon Foster's

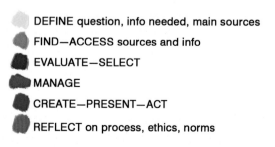

Figure 4.1 Information palette.

comparison of the information process with an artist's palette, in that its range of activities remains available during information seeking (Foster, 2004).

The titles of the different components of the information palette have been adjusted to capture essential information qualities and practices, especially in relation to transliteracy.

- *DEFINE question, information needed, and main sources* relates to the conscious understanding, which takes a person into a particular direction in the information process. It is based on identification of an information need.
- *FIND AND ACCESS sources and relevant information* captures the search process, in which relevant information may be found in a range of sources. Finding the sources and relevant information is a part of the process, but so is an ability to access them. Access has been clearly identified here as it relates to the study findings pointing to the significance of access conditions and understanding of social contexts surrounding information access.
- *EVALUATE-SELECT* refers to evaluation as a well-recognized aspect of the process, but it also brings to the fore selection. Valuable information may or may not be selected for a number of reasons, which may be related to considerations other than the quality of information. Selection decisions need to be a distinct part of a holistic understanding of the process and conscious information strategy.
- *MANAGE* is about organizing information based on content, technical, and any other relevant characteristics. The word "manage" has been chosen instead of "organize" as it better captures the potential complexity of working with information.
- *CREATE-PRESENT-ACT* is about various forms of information use to create new information, understanding, and knowledge; combining existing information elements for presentation purposes; and about the use of information to inform decisions and action.
- *REFLECT* is part of the process in which individuals and groups reflect on the process, ethics, norms, and personal meanings. Reflection comes at the beginning of the information process as people think and realize an information need, throughout the process as they decide about the next step, and at the end of the process to evaluate and understand recent experience. In educational contexts, it is important to embed reflection as a formal part of any inquiry.
- *HOLISTIC UNDERSTANDING* of the process is indicated by the idea of the palette rather than individual colors. It emphasizes the importance of understanding the information process and its components as a whole.

Form palette (Fig. 4.2) captures "forms" that shape interactions with information.

- *EXPERIENCE* is about opportunities to act, sense, and think through a range of different experiences such as writing a story, performing, reading, and working visually.
- *MEDIA* relates to the use of different media formats (e.g., book, video, database).
- *COMMUNICATION* is about using different forms of communication through different channels in a variety of genres, languages, and for different audiences.
- *COLLABORATION* is about working with others formally and informally face to face, online, and in blended environments.
- *CITIZENSHIP* refers to understanding of a range of social issues, which determine successful participation in information environments. It includes legal, normative, cultural, and ethical issues. Copyright, plagiarism, and appropriate online behavior as they are commonly taught in educational settings are part of this "form."

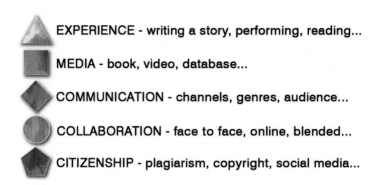

Figure 4.2 Form palette.

The transliteracy palette (Fig. 4.3) consists of both information and form palettes, and offers the ability to mix them in many different combinations. If context is a frame, information and form palettes provide materials to create a transliterate design. Learning to apply different colors to many different forms in a range of different situations is a way to develop transliteracy.

4.2.2 Transliteracy curriculum mapping

Formal teaching and learning are organized around curricula and measurable outcomes. The coordinated development of students' knowledge and skills in formal education depends on the integration of these skills in the everyday practice of teaching and learning. When a learning area is missing from teaching documents and measurable outcomes, there is no mechanism to monitor its implementation in practice. That area of learning is destined to take a back seat every time there is a pressing demand on the teacher's time to achieve prescribed outcomes and complete administrative tasks. Without an insight into the content of teaching across the board, it is difficult to know whether there is a need to unclutter and remove duplication to create space and time for new content.

As illustrated with transliteracy palettes, integration of transliteracy depends on integration of information capabilities in a variety of ways. Some schools and individual teachers integrate key capabilities, which constitute transliteracy, better than the others, many do it with enthusiasm and talent, achieving excellent results. However, outcomes for individual students often depend on the teacher they happen to have. Even more arbitrary is the development of an ability to apply skills across different contexts. There is no guarantee students would learn all the critical transliteracy skills during their time in formal education unless there is a system in place to track students' progress from one classroom to another and, ideally, from one school to another. Very few learning areas are more important for life and work in the information age than information and ICT capabilities, yet very few important skills are taught in a more haphazard way. The main reason is that education, especially secondary and tertiary, is based on subject or discipline specialization

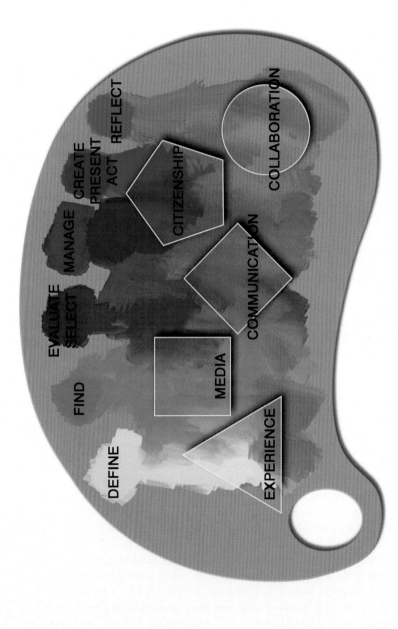

Figure 4.3 Transliteracy palettes.

whereas information, ICT capabilities, communication and collaboration, creativity and critical thinking are not subject-specific. These capabilities need to be developed in all subject areas.

Transliteracy is a core literacy with application in all subjects and learning areas. It can and should be taught in individual subjects, but its real implementation is cross-disciplinary as learners find different ways to connect disparate areas of their learning. Its broad coverage is an opportunity and a challenge for formal education. At the same time, the broad transliteracy framework opens up many opportunities for new connections, provides a flexible approach to implement new technologies and pedagogical interests as they arise, and encompasses key modern literacies within a unifying and purposeful transliteracy framework.

A good start for the implementation of transliteracy in formal education is a definition of the concept and outcomes for different educational stages. Many universities already have aspects of information and digital literacy integrated in their graduate outcomes and some have done considerable amounts of work on integrating information literacy into their discipline-based courses. For schools, national curricula define literacy outcomes for primary and secondary education. Bush (2012) observes that transliteracy is implicitly present in the Common Core Standards. This is also the case with the new Australian Curriculum. Existing curricular documents and tools for schools provide some direction for transliteracy as long as they are used as flexible guides rather than finite prescriptions. A major educational challenge, however, is to ensure that good general plans are implemented in practice. A large proportion of documents used in the education are guides, standards, and plans, rather than records of what is happening in the classroom.

Curriculum mapping is an appropriate method we currently have to make sure that plans are implemented. It is a well-established approach to bridging a gap between a plan and its reality. "A curriculum map is a working document that illustrates exactly what is taking place in classrooms. Maps reveal what is being taught over the course of a year, within a unit of study, and even down to a specific lesson" (ASCD, 2006, p. 3). Lynn Erickson points out that curriculum mapping addresses key questions: "Who is doing what? How does our work align with our goals? Are we operating efficiently and effectively?' (Jacobs, 2004, p. v). In the same book (edited by Jacobs), Truesdale, Thompson, and Lucas consider the potential of curriculum mapping for building a learning community.

Curriculum mapping has been used in schools for about two decades, but it has also attracted the interest of university educators as they have looked for ways to ensure the development of graduate capabilities and track generic and transferable skills in teaching and learning. A number of universities, as well as individual schools, faculties, and academic libraries used curriculum mapping to ensure that objectives are implemented in practice (Willett, 2008; Oliver et al., 2010; Spencer et al., 2012; Buchanan et al., 2015).

A possible pitfall is that curriculum mapping can become an administrative tool for focusing on outcomes and quality assurance, rather than on individual learners and their needs. Wang (2015) warned that curriculum mapping tends to have a vocational orientation in that it helps students to include ranges of skills required for particular jobs, rather than preparing them to navigate an unpredictable life and teaching them independence. Wang proposes a rhizomatic (as proposed by Deleuze and Guattari) instead of a hierarchical, arborescent approach, stressing that learning can grow from any node, not only via charted pathways:

> *In applying curricular practices, teachers are invited to connect, both with the global environment and with learners' inner selves. By knowing the world, students open their minds and expand their lives. Students should not only be successful in tracing an entrepreneurial self; receiving a higher education has the potential to free them from a pre-designed self by mapping the self in other ways. Therefore, the purpose of curriculum mapping is to educate a cartographer to create his or her new life.*
>
> *Wang, 2015, pp. 1557–1558*

In order to ensure the development of transliteracy, it needs to become an integral part of formal education as well as to branch out in many other directions. Prescriptive documents and open-ended learning both have their places in education. Curriculum mapping, I believe, can be very useful for transliteracy, both as an arborescent and as a rhizomatic approach.

Curriculum mapping of transliteracy skills aims to make sure, firstly, that the main skills are being taught, and secondly, that students have opportunities to "move across." In an arborescent structure of curriculum mapping, following the structure of the curriculum, this means learning across the curricular content, experimenting with a wide range of media, technologies, and genres, with opportunities for cross-disciplinary application of knowledge and skills. Using a rhizomatic perspective, the emphasis is on the student's and the educator's recognition of personal meanings and learning that happens outside the classroom and school space. Individual projects, which connect with a range of student experiences and interests, provide opportunities for students to explore less structured approaches and to use mapping as a tool of reflection. Schools, libraries, youth, and special-interest groups can all use maps to chart and scaffold individual learning journeys.

With a curriculum map, a school or faculty has an understanding of what is happening across the board. It provides an opportunity to identify areas of shared interest and variations in meanings, and to highlight gaps and overlaps in learning. The next step is to think about students and their needs to see what sort of "mixing and matching" is required to enable the learning of transliteracy. The aim is to focus on particular areas for development and use the transliteracy palettes to ensure many combinations of information and form palettes across a wide range of different contexts.

This way of thinking about learning is supported by educational research and practice as well as the application of educational insights to the field of information literacy. Bruce et al. (2006, p. 6), for example, pointed out the variation theory, which "proposes that learning occurs when variations in ways of understanding or experiencing are discerned." They give examples of learning music by discerning different sounds and learning information searching when it is experienced in different ways. "Bringing about learning through widening experience, and thus revealing variation, is the underlying principle." Similarly, the experience of interacting with information in many different ways, applying skills in novel situations, and reflecting on the process enhances an ability to deal with information in novel situations in the future.

Embedding transliteracy at St. Vincent's College: curriculum mapping

At St. Vincent's College we have done some preliminary work to prepare for embedding transliteracy in teaching and learning. These are some milestones we have achieved, not necessarily in this order:

- A draft of transliteracy objectives and outcomes for each high school stage presented to the HODs for an initial consultation. Objectives and outcomes were developed with the idea of backward design, in which the final outcome is determined first.
- An exercise in marking common topics for one year group and discussions about cross-overs.
- A pilot project to map transferable skills in Semester 1, Year 7 (the first year of high school in Australia).
- A sample grid showing how transliteracy is integrated in a teaching unit (Table 4.1).
- The transliteracy grid shared with departments to start mapping.
- Opening discussions: Presentations of transliteracy and research findings to teachers; experience with the French Transliteracy Project, and relevant scope and sequence for the unit shared by the French teacher.

Pilot project. Additional explanation is needed to highlight some details of the pilot project to map transferable skills in Year 7. It started with a clear rationale and a problem statement related to the best interests of students against the background of requirements of the new Australian Curriculum and a sense of compartmentalized teaching practices. The scope and methodology were identified in advance. Heads of departments used a shared spreadsheet to plot topics, and subject-specific and transferable skills taught in the first semester in Year 7. A working group consisting of teaching staff with different areas of expertise analyzed and coded responses. Four categories of transferable skills emerged from data analysis:

1. Rules and practices
2. Study skills
3. Thinking skills
4. Communication skills.

The absence of some skills was also noted as part of analysis. The group provided some recommendations for further work in this area, including

(Continued on page 96)

Table 4.1 Transliteracy grid

Subject: French

Year: 10

Topic: School life

Overall task: Compare Australian and French school life; record a conversational video; use your research to write a letter to the Principal with recommendations for change or design a poster to promote your school. You can use an augmented reality app to combine your poster with video

	Experience	IT & Media	Communication	Collaboration	Citizenship
Define	– Conversation with a French exchange student and teacher – Reading magazine articles – Searching online	– Websites – Magazines – Textbooks – Images – Edmodo (online chat for schools)	Discussions in groups and pairs, face to face and online	– In pairs to prepare videos – With other students to solve IT issues, share images & info	– Online interactions (Edmodo, "following" other users on the app Aurasma) – Images under copyright
Find & access	– Taking photos – Finding relevant information online	– Print sources – Aurasma – Camera – Computer			
Evaluate&Select	– Individual and in pairs—select focus and sources				
Manage	– Organizing digital and analog sources	– Files and folders on computer – Download images from camera – Sources on Aurasma – Change file types	– With another team member and teacher		

	Experience	IT & Media	Communication	Collaboration	Citizenship
Create/Present/ Act	– Writing (video script; letter, etc.) – Performance for video recording – Video editing – Visual presentation of a poster/letter, etc.	– Camera – Video editing software – Aurasma	– With an audience (at school and outside when videos are published on the website)		– Presenting appropriate content to the Principal & online – Authorship – Acknowledging sources
Reflect	– Watching all videos and providing feedback to other students – Completing survey – Participation in class discussion for the transliteracy study	– Online surveys (evaluation of other students' videos and survey about the experience)	– With researcher and the class	– Participate in research	– Appropriate way of expressing opinion about experience in the class; giving feedback to other students – Privacy in research

> **(cont'd from page 93)**
>
> a need to establish common terminology. Findings were summarized as follows:
>
> *The pilot revealed that curriculum mapping has a significant potential in revealing similarities across subject areas and gaps in skill development. Grouping of data indicated potential areas for further investigation with implications for informing curriculum planning within and across disciplines, and enhancing classroom practice. HODs and other teachers appeared to be interested in the process. Although some team members had reservations about the value of curriculum mapping, they started to believe in its potential by the end of the pilot.*
>
> **Mapping on the transliteracy grid.** Some time was required for the introduction of transliteracy as a way of thinking about classroom practice, to allow teachers to adjust and process information. The Languages Department found it easier to accept since they had already completed a transliteracy project. Table 4.1 illustrates a transliteracy grid, using the French Transliteracy Project as an example.

4.3   Pedagogies for transliteracy

Many student-centered pedagogies are congruent with transliteracy, which is developed through a range of learning experiences in thinking, interacting, and acting across the information field. Teaching methods for inquiry-, project-, problem- and phenomenon-based learning, multiliteracy and connected learning are particularly well suited for transliteracy, but other approaches may be suitable as well. The guiding principle is the ultimate aim: to empower and equip students to face new situations in the increasingly complex information world with resourcefulness, creativity, and understanding.

4.3.1   Inquiry-, project-, and phenomenon-based learning

The value of project- and inquiry-based learning has been well recognized in educational theory and practice. This type of learning promotes critical thinking and engagement with real-life issues and topics of student interest, and encourages exploration and meaningful interactions with information, while tapping into numerous skills required to progress through the project. Aspects of the information process are so critical for inquiry-based learning that they are often integrated to the extent that they become invisible as discrete information skills. Hobbs (2011) identifies essential dimensions of digital and media literacy—access, analyze, create, reflect, act—and sees them in terms of digital rather than information literacy. It may be a useful way of thinking about digital literacy, but from the transliteracy perspective, it is important to keep an awareness of key skill sets. Identifying information with digital capabilities may lead to a neglect of one capability and exclusion of analog technologies, which may be appropriately combined with digital technologies. In working with teachers, librarians may need to point out how some capabilities are part of transliteracy, but teachers who are experienced in guiding inquiry-based learning would easily understand the significance of information capability. In addition to this, school librarians have gained significant experience with the guided inquiry (The Center for International Scholarship in School Libraries, 2016), an approach grounded in Carol Kuhlthau's research, which can be successfully used to teach transliteracy.

Phenomenon-based learning takes project-based learning a step further. It is an integral part of the Finnish education reform (Sahlberg, 2015; Halinen, 2016), which recognizes the need to align education with broader societal changes. Once the Finnish reform is adopted, phenomenon-based learning will happen during assigned class time when students will engage in cross-disciplinary investigation of real-life issues. Students will be involved in planning and assessing their learning. As Sahlberg explains, phenomenon-based learning is a continuation of a tradition of holistic teaching in Finnish classrooms. At the time of writing this book, the Finnish reform has not been implemented yet, but it will be interesting to learn about its development. From the description and existing experience with project-based and inquiry-based learning, it appears a very good approach for the development of transliteracy and a step further in ensuring cross-disciplinary approaches in education.

4.3.2 Multiliteracy and multimodality

The theory and practice of multiliteracy can provide some useful ideas and tools for a transliterate classroom. Although their roots, frames, and foci are different, transliteracy and multiliteracy share some common themes (The New London Group defined its multiliteracies manifesto in Cazden et al., 1996). Multimodality, engagement with technologies, and interest in a variety of texts, situated learning and critical reflection are elements which connect transliteracy with the concept of multiliteracy.

Tools and techniques for connecting different modalities and genres are particularly useful for transliteracy. "Dance a thesis" competitions have produced some entertaining, clever, and educational work around the world. Visualization provides some fascinating examples of transfers between modalities. Infographics and the concept of beautiful information at the site http://www.informationisbeautiful.net illustrates how artistic visual devices and communication techniques can be used to present a range of messages, including the communication of scientific and statistical information. Technologies for manipulating sound bring a visual aspect to the auditory experience. Similarly, music has been made on the basis of patterns in scientific data. An Australian couple, Fran and Jacques Soddell, for example, produced electronic music based on a computer analysis of fungal growth. Music technology students in Lupton's study related to sound by understanding "aural information (what the sound sounds like) and affective information (the feeling that the sound evokes, e.g., an eerie feeling)" as well as the visual presentation of the sound (Lupton, 2008, p. 71). This comment is related to the experience of an academic described in the study on transliteracy who thought of access to auditory information in terms of different sets of metadata, sound, and visual representation of sound waves. In these examples, technology aids a sense of synesthesia as a lived and embodied experience rather than an abstract idea.

Cooper et al. (2013) conducted a study into multiliteracy and reported that students found making news with technology different from their regular English classes. A possible explanation may be related to Pang and Marton's conjecture "that new meanings are acquired from experiencing differences against a background of sameness, rather than experiencing sameness against a background of differences" (Pang and Marton, 2013, p. 1065). It may be that their conjecture relates to student perception of transliterate learning as a novel experience in the sense that transliteracy as movement "across" stands out against a more unified background of classroom experiences.

4.3.3   Teaching "moving across"

Inquiry-based learning and the development of multiliteracy may not be part of regular classroom practice, but they are not foreign ideas in most contemporary schools. More challenging pedagogies are those that try to bridge a gap between traditionally separate areas of learning.

Education and academic work are based on divisions between disciplines, curricular and personal interests, feeling and thinking, creativity and analysis. Transliterate "movement across," on the other hand, requires the whole field. While there is a value in working within one area and developing a single skill, transliteracy cannot thrive within persistent boundaries. Lehmans and Mazurier (2015, p. 313) found that their research into transliteracy "points out the transformation of learning strategies in collaborative situations, transfers between informal personal digital abilities and formal academic skills and between experts and novices, transition from learning to creating and from creating to learning, cognitive redistribution between spaces."

4.3.3.1   Connected learning

A significant obstacle to holistic approaches to learning is a rather persistent disconnection between learning inside and outside school or university. Students spend a considerable time in formal education, but they spend even more time outside school. During that time, young people talk to family and friends in person, online and by phone, play games, instruments and sport, read, draw, do some housework, watch TV, and experiment with digital content creation. In these activities, they learn and use information most of the time, but connections between formal and informal learning seem to happen only occasionally. Lehmans and Mazurier (2015, p. 317) studied the evidence of connection between personal information use and learning at school and found that students "do not easily use their personal skills and do not 'naturally' make bridges between their private uses and academic demands." Both students and teachers "tend to install strong barriers between private life and cognitive process at school, which limits the range of knowledge formats that can be used at school" (Lehmans and Cordier, 2014, p. 126).

> Australian high school students spend approximately six hours a day at school, five days a week during approximately forty weeks of school time per year, including public holidays. If they sleep eight hours a day, they spend nearly five times more waking hours outside school than at school. Even if three hours are added to every school day for homework and school-based extracurricular activities, there are three times more waking hours left for nonschool activities.

A recognition of this situation and its implications for student engagement and the quality of learning inspired the development of the idea of connected learning: "It advocates for broadened access to learning that is socially embedded, interest driven, and oriented toward educational, economic, or political opportunity" (Ito et al., 2013, p. 4). The authors recognize that "(y)oung people need connection and translation between in-school and out-of-school learning" (p. 46) and suggest strategies to bridge the gap. Similarly, Hobbs (2011) would like to see learning environments in which students can be part of and contributors to the community. Her advice is to connect the classroom to the world, support leadership and collaboration, and develop integrity and accountability. Lehmans and Cordier (2014, p. 119) note that "(p)orosity between school life and private life, personal history and social practices, is associated with porosity between areas of expertise..." They identified strategies to support transliteracy and suggested that the "transliteracy approach to information activity in education allows the emergence of an information maturity associated with the construction of knowledge, according to a 'grammar of usage'" (p. 126). Connected learning is a major enabler of transliteracy. With its orientation toward lifelong learning and life demands, transliteracy development can only benefit from being guided and practiced outside school.

4.3.3.2   Emotion, cognition, and creativity

A sense of personal connection involves engagement on cognitive and emotional levels that opens another territory of disconnection. "The cultivation of feeling has long been marginalized by academic education... The conventional academic curriculum largely ignores the importance of developing the 'soft skills' such as an ability to listen and to empathize. This is not a coincidence or an oversight. It is a structural feature of academicism," wrote Robinson (2011, pp. 177−178) in relation to creativity in education. The evidence for the importance of emotion in information processing and learning has grown in recent decades (Damasio, 2000a, 2000b; Weiss, 2000; Dalgleish, 2002; Scherer, 2002; Kaluzniacky, 2004; Lacewing, 2004; Nahl and Bilal, 2007; Bowen, 2014). It is still unclear how exactly emotion and cognition work together, but the conclusion that they interact in multiple ways cannot be denied on the basis of existing research (Robinson et al., 2013). The leaders of the Finnish educational reform, again, recognize the importance of emotion for learning and specifically address its inclusion (Halinen, 2016). From the transliteracy perspective, construction of personal meaning, self-reflection, creativity, and working with others are not possible without acknowledgment and integration of emotion in learning. Furthermore, the ability to move across the cognitive-emotional division is a basis for deeper insights and work in different knowledge domains.

Closely aligned with the separation between cognition and emotion is that between analytical thinking and creativity. Analytical thinking has been the main area of educational work for centuries, while creativity has often stayed on the margins of mainstream educational interests. This is partially because the social value of creativity may be less obvious, perhaps because creativity was often seen as an innate attribute of talented individuals. However, contemporary views of creativity are moving away from both the idea of its being less visible or valuable to the society and its being the result mainly of personal talent. Csikszentmihalyi (1988) argues that creativity cannot exist outside social and historical contexts, pointing toward the importance of societal influences in addition to individual abilities. Innovation, as a social construct with significant value in modern economy, is related to creativity. Robinson considers creativity as one of the main elements of innovation:

> *In practice, a culture of innovation depends on cultivating three processes, each of which is related to the others. (p. 219)*
>
> • *The first is imagination: the ability to bring to mind events and ideas that are not present to our senses.*
>
> • *The second is creativity: the process of having original ideas that have value.*
>
> • *The third is innovation: the process of putting original ideas into practice.*
>
> *Robinson, 2011, pp. 219–220*

The value of original ideas is socially determined and so is the process of putting creativity in to practice. Zhao (2012) considers creativity to be a key aspect of successful education for participation in the future economy. Considering the importance of innovation for the economic success of nations and individuals, it is understandable why the development of creativity is increasingly of interest to many groups, not only educators.

Discussions about creativity in educational and organizational theory revolve around the view that everyone has some creative ability that can be developed.

Cropley (2001) identifies six components of educational environments which foster creativity: divergent thinking; a general knowledge and thinking base; a specific knowledge base and specific skills; focusing and task commitment; motives and motivation; and openness and tolerance of ambiguity. Embedded in these components are investigative and independent learning, playfulness, and support for fantasy and imagination. Components of an educational environment which support creativity are also beneficial for transliteracy.

All previously mentioned pedagogies, which can support transliteracy, are congruent with the development of creativity. As a framework based on establishing connections and moving across epistemic and technological contexts, transliteracy provides a fertile environment for holistic pedagogical approaches. Free movement across the fields is required to develop transliteracy, which, in turn, provides conditions for deepening connections between traditionally disparate ways of knowing.

4.3.4 In the classroom

With all the opportunities young people have in environments rich with information and technology, formal educational settings are still critically important. First, it is easy to assume that young people have already gained all the digital and information skills they need in their private lives, but this is not the case. The notion of "digital natives" who know everything important about digital environments has been repeatedly debunked, as mentioned in the first two chapters of this book. Secondly, socioeconomic differences among student families have an impact not only on educational outcomes in general, but on digital skills as well. Hargittai (2010) found that race, gender, and parents' education influence variations in the Internet skills of 18- to 30-year-old study participants. If these skills are not systematically taught at school, the divisions can only become more significant. Thirdly, when it comes to formal learning, students consistently rely on institutional authority in selecting resources (Lea and Jones, 2011). It may sound counterintuitive, considering the problems with plagiarism and low-quality sources used in many assignments, but teachers and librarians can confirm that most students at least try to follow authoritative advice about information use, providing that they know how to locate reliable sources in the first place. Lea and Jones invited teachers to make sure a range of texts is being used and to pay attention to the whole learning process, not only the outcomes in the form of final assignments. A conversation between a student and a librarian about the suitability of different sorts of information can go a long way in teaching the student how to evaluate information for academic purposes and understand the value of nonacademic resources for current topics (Megwalu, 2014). Cooper et al. (2013) found that teacher technology skills, the integration of technology, and effective learning scaffolds are most important for the effective achievement of multiliteracy outcomes.

The experience with transliteracy at St. Vincent's College confirms the relevance of information advice pointing toward the importance of bringing the whole school on board with transliteracy, to actively promote and support collaboration between departments, and teachers and librarians. The insights from work at the college provide some practical clues about what works for transliteracy. Study findings from the previous chapter offer insights into the inner workings of transliteracy in practice, but it is worth summarizing some aspects that proved to be successful in the classroom.

Timing is important. Many schools that take project-based learning seriously block out longer periods of time for it. iTell was rescued from its shaky start once the program was moved from a one-hour after-school time slot, spread across the term, to a more compact whole day schedule. Whole day sessions for part of the program were appreciated by students in the Enrichment program. Whole days are not always necessary or even desirable, but a longer session at the beginning of a program is useful to set the tone and initiate student connections around the content.

Space and the way it is used matter. Students were repeatedly saying how they liked working in the library, as it was a different space from the classroom. It is true, but it matters that the room was used more freely, as students could use the whole library and sit wherever they liked. Sitting under tall tables with a laptop worked for some of them. Space and tools for collaboration are important, but so is space for distance.

Rules and spontaneity are both needed. A transliterate way of working is new to most students. Setting the rules and expectations is important for a sense of security, trust, and shared understanding of its aim, but so is a sense of flexibility, playfulness, and connection.

Playfulness and a sense of surprise are irreplaceable in setting the tone. They ignite wonder and open pathways to creativity.

Team teaching is advisable. Transliteracy work is enjoyable for students and teaching staff but requires nimble and resourceful staff who can think quickly and laterally. Guiding lots of individual projects, especially when they are cross-disciplinary and require significant use of technology, is time-intensive for teaching staff. This is why transliteracy projects are best done in teams that tap into different types of staff expertise and can provide individual attention to students. In my experience so far, transliterate projects have always been opportunities to build a sense of a learning community as students and teachers all come together as learners in some way. As discussed in the previous chapters, students enjoyed a sense of being in a learning community in which they fed off each other's ideas and benefited from the competent guidance of the adults. The same can be said about librarians and teachers, who gained insights from everyone's ideas, but felt they particularly benefited from learning from and with their colleagues.

Tools and resources do not have to be expensive, but they need to be available and suited for the purpose. We used laptops and mainly free software for specialized tasks in all projects. A variety of information and appreciation that it is coming from different sources is important. Students who talk about their projects outside class, share information, advice, and stories, and run their ideas by teaching staff learn many valuable lessons about the information process while gaining social, technological, and content-related skills and insights. A sense that education is multifarious gains strength in the process of collaborative transliterate learning from sources of different quality and provenance, regardless of the setting. Even an experienced historian like Peter Read felt that access to diverse knowledge is something extraordinary as he admired the traditional knowledge of an Indigenous scholar.

The "human library," a relatively new library service which allows clients to "borrow" people from the community and learn from their experiences, has an objective of promoting the sharing of experiences, expertise, and community knowledge and connections. Schools also acknowledge different types of knowledge and authority by inviting people outside education into the classroom or by taking students on excursions where they can develop a sense that there are many different sources of valuable information.

There are many classrooms in which teachers employ similar methods to those used in transliteracy projects. It is likely that they achieve similar results. But it is important to remember that what seems to matter in transliteracy is a whole picture, rather than particular teaching methods and techniques. It is worth keeping in mind students' perceptions that their experiences with transliteracy projects are significantly different from their regular classroom experiences. The perception was also recorded in the groups, which had the same teacher, the usual timing of the lessons and formal assessment, pointing toward transliteracy as a point of difference. With transliteracy as a dynamic pattern of new combinations and connections developed for real people in their unique contexts, it can be expected that transliteracy will keep offering fresh experiences, but "moving across" will become a habit of the mind.

4.4   Transliterate reading and writing[1]

Reading and writing are key learning and information practices in the Western world. A great deal of information is accessed through reading and communicated in writing. Learning to read and write is instrumental in becoming a literate person, an educational goal over centuries. Both skills were typically learned in formal education, and practiced by using pen, paper, and printed material. Recent technological developments have changed the situation which, with some variations, has persisted through centuries. We now read throughout the day from paper, mobile devices, and computers, and write more than ever before in various ways. It is hardly surprising that the impact of technology on our reading and writing has become a topic of common interest. Stories about the effect of digital technology on reading and education have become regular features in the media, concerns about our diminished ability to focus on reading are frequently raised in blogs and academic writing, while social media provide a daily offering of pictures and videos of babies and pets "reading" from various devices. Businesses have seized the opportunity by offering new methods and software to amplify reading experiences and abilities at any age. It is often difficult, even for experienced library and educational professionals, to distinguish the hype from the hard evidence. Before proceeding to transliterate reading and writing, it is worth considering research findings on the topic of reading and writing in the digital world.

[1] This section is based on the paper "Transliterate reading" (Sukovic, 2015).

Most concerns are related to reading, as the more fundamental of the two practices. Questions arising from the proliferation of digital reading devices could be roughly grouped into two categories: (1) questions around the suitability of the screen for print-based types of reading and (2) questions about the emergence of new reading practices and behaviors. An overwhelming proportion of current discussions belongs in the first category. A critical issue in these discussions concerns the impact of the screens we use daily on the quantity and quality of our reading.

Despite a common assumption that people nowadays read fewer books than they did in the past, American and Australian studies (Rainie et al., 2012; Australia Council for the Arts, 2014) have found that the opposite is true, although these findings are not definitive. According to Australian studies by Roy Morgan Research (2014, July 21; Roy Morgan Research, 2016, May 10) book reading is declining, but online activities do not seem to distract people from reading books. People who spend more time on the Internet also spend more hours reading, a study found (Roy Morgan Research, 2014, July 21). The latest research of readership in the United States shows a fall in book reading since 2011, but it remains statistically even with findings in 2012 (Rainie and Perrin, 2015). In order to put these trends in perspective, reading in the United States has increased significantly since the 1950s and research shows that access to digital content has affected an increase in overall reading by people in younger age groups (Baron, 2015).

Studies of the quality of reading as a focused activity generally favor paper, while electronic text is preferred for searching and skim reading. Although this is a trend, it is often difficult to compare findings. Most studies rely on participants' self-report and, when testing is involved, it is usually impossible to compare the results of different studies because of their different designs. Contradictory findings also indicate that reading is a multifaceted and contextual activity. Recent studies (Stoop et al., 2013; Chen et al., 2014) confirm well-recognized advantages of tablets and e-readers, that they can carry a large number of texts, are instantly searchable, and can be skim read easily. On the other hand, physical interactions with hard copies, the stability of print text, ease of browsing, and nonlinear reading all aid immersed reading, comprehension, and learning (Hillesund, 2010; Mangen and Kuiken, 2014). There are plenty of opportunities for distraction while reading online, so it is hardly surprising that participants in Baron's study (2015) reported that they were significantly more likely to multitask when reading on screen. However, reading from screen on its own may not hinder comprehension. Margolin et al. (2013) compared comprehension after reading different text types on computer, e-reader, and paper and found no significant difference. Similarly, Chen and Catrambone (2015) found no difference in comprehension after reading from screen and paper under test conditions. A study of narrative engagement found that reading from a tablet negatively affected the reader's engagement when text was perceived as nonfiction, but the effect was not observed when text was perceived as fiction (Mangen and Kuiken, 2014). It is possible that the habit of skim reading factual texts online was behind participants' reading the text differently when they thought the story described a real event. Chen et al. (2014) reported that reading from paper improved literal (also called "shallow") comprehension, but the difference was less significant for deep comprehension, especially when participants were familiar with tablets. A study by the National Literacy Trust in the United Kingdom found that electronic devices have advantages in improving the reading habits of some groups of children and noted a general preference among young people for reading from screen (Picton, 2014). An Australian study, however, found that teenagers do not necessarily prefer e-books to paper books (Merga, 2014).

Reading and writing often go together, especially in the practice of note taking during reading. A large student survey indicated a preference for reading on paper, especially because of the ease of annotation and highlighting (Vandenhoek, 2013). Familiarity with digital tools may be an issue, but it is not the only reason for the preference. In the Vandenhoek's study, around half of the participants indicated they knew how to highlight on screen, but only 29% used this feature, while 70% took notes on paper, while reading on screen. Mueller and Oppenheimer (2014) found that copious and verbatim notes taken on laptops are associated with shallower information processing while hand-written, summarized notes are better for conceptual understanding. They interpret their study findings as an indication that notes taken on laptops may even impair learning. Another study found that transcription on laptops can be beneficial for recall, particularly for people with poor working memory (Bui et al., 2013). Studies like this indicate that different note-taking techniques may be appropriate for different people and purposes, but it seems advisable to include summarized hand-written notes at some point in the learning process.

People's comfort and their perceptions of the usefulness of different technologies are important when considering the advantages and disadvantages of different modes of reading and writing. A series of studies on perceptions of reading and writing, conducted in several European countries, provides some comparable results as the researchers used the same study design. University students were asked to write essays about their experiences of reading and writing with pen and paper compared with keyboard and computer. The initial study conducted in Italy (Fortunati and Vincent, 2014) found that students perceived writing on paper as a more free, personal, and creative activity. It can be done on any surface, it supports exploratory and creative responses, such as doodling, and handwriting provides information about personality and the moment of writing. Students also appreciated the possibility of "augmented writing" on computer with access to dictionaries, hyperlinking, and the advantages of text manipulation and use of other digital tools. Reading preferences depended on the material and purpose—the computer is preferred for short texts and purposeful reading in which digital tools can be used. Paper is preferred for focused reading. A study in Germany, the United Kingdom, and Italy confirmed the key findings of the initial Italian study with no indication of major cultural differences (Farinosi et al., 2016). Paper—screen, pen—keyboard were not seen as opposites by study participants for whom the choice depended on situation and purpose. Handwriting was perceived as a slower process, which allows better processing and supports learning, but the advantages of digital writing were noted too. Overall, the conclusion was that analog and digital technologies exist and are used side by side. It is common that people draw on paper, scan, and share digitally.

Some differences were found in a study conducted in Finland, where students have been more immersed in the digital world (Taipale, 2014). While students' descriptions of their reading habits were similar to those seen in other studies, digital writing had the default status when the Finns compared handwriting with electronic text. They appreciated writing by hand for the same reasons as others, but emphasized the advantages of fast writing with a keyboard as they could follow their thoughts more quickly and modify text more easily. When it came to the physical aspects of reading, the Finns preferred to work with pen and paper, as these technologies are more adaptable to different situations and bodily positions (Taipale, 2015). In considering the pros and cons of different technologies, none of the studies provided the evidence that digital media could replace the rich communication enabled by the use of pen and paper.

Research into the suitability of new technologies for existing reading and writing practices points toward the importance of both analog and digital technologies to meet a range of needs and requirements. However, the transfer of existing behaviors and practices into the new environment is only one focal point. Another must be concerned with the emergence of new qualities of reading and writing, if we are to understand the nature of a significant cultural shift.

Reading from screen and paper: transliteracy study

Scholar

Some of the research practices described by the academics in the transliteracy study are skim reading of search results and a large number of texts, printing for more convenient reading and intellectual assimilation, and remixing passages from a textual collection in novel approaches. Skim reading was usually performed on screen to assess the usefulness of retrieved information before more focused reading. Some scholars mentioned speed reading a whole novel on screen, while a few participants practiced reading from screen even when they read in a more focused way and for extended periods of time.

Printing for in-depth reading or speed reading of longer texts was common, as most people found reading from screen very tiring. Some researchers preferred to take printouts home to read in an armchair rather than at their desk and talked about different physical settings required for focused reading. Frequent interruptions at work were not conducive to focused reading. Another reason for printing was to aid the intellectual assimilation of material. Participant 2/1, for example, felt that she had not read the text properly if she read it on screen, while Participant 13/1 needed to make printouts at some point for synthesis, because it was easy to keep adding electronic files without any intellectual grasp of that material. The printed text was usually marked and annotated.

Working simultaneously with hard and electronic copies was a way of using time in an archive efficiently. Participant 7/1 described how she worked in overseas archives, where she would conduct a catalog search and save it for a

(Continued)

(cont'd)

day, and then she would start ordering materials in hard copies. While waiting for the hard copies to arrive, she used a digitized version to make printouts. Participant 6/1 worked in a similar way by printing digitized rather than archival hard copies. In these examples, the reading of digital copies for assessment, examination of originals when the content and physical aspects of the document were of interest, and subsequent reading of page images were all part of a process in which the reading of electronic copies and originals have their specific purposes. One scholar described his practice of reading the text of an archival document into a tape recorder when photocopying was not allowed.

Community

For research fields based on scattered evidence and knowledge situated outside well-established institutions, search engines enable a deeper reading than codex. The website *A History of Aboriginal Sydney* offers hundreds of images and videos as well as some textual overviews and interactive tools to present parts of a dispersed history and enable their discovery. During the project, team members were considering and learning new ways of presenting textual information online and combining it with images and videos. In the process, they were discovering different possibilities for reading the material—in a broad sense of the word. By answering numerous questions and comments from website users, the team was learning about community interest and how historical memories presented online connected with users' personal stories. Peter Read commented on user reading of the research data:

> You'd be able to make all those links yourself, which is what we historians do and put it together and say, 'I know the history of Sydney, even if it's not on this website, I understand it differently now. I've got a certain feeling from it, from that website. I can use all information again, not just because it's a big encyclopaedia, but because it presents a certain view that I can make the connections between them.'

Another team member commented that no user of the site would watch several hundreds of videos and read all the material:

> So everyone is going to form a different picture. And it will always happen because you will always bring your own mind into something, but in a different way from reading a book ... People are going to just dip in and take what they want ... There are underlying themes to get a felt sense of what is going on. Whatever you explore, somebody is going to tell you one particular perspective. (Chantal Jackson)

Julie Janson, an Indigenous researcher on the team with strong connections with the Indigenous community in Sydney, commented on the importance of presenting history online and the sense of user engagement:

> When I introduce people to it and they have a look, they ring me up and say, 'Oh, my God, that was extraordinary! I stayed up all night looking at all these stories, and the way it was easy to interact, and between the different sections, and the

(Continued)

(cont'd)

galleries and video galleries.' And I had nothing but very excited feedback from Aboriginal community.

Teenager

Creative reading was at the core of *iTell* as students explored new approaches to their favorite texts through digital storytelling. An interesting aspect of iTell was a collaborative reading and construction of meaning. Collaboration emerged with a group of Indigenous students who created a pastiche comprised of individual memories about events affecting their community. They used newspaper articles, drawings, digital images, voiceover, and sound effects to relate personal memories to a publicly known story and present it as a collaborative interpretation of events. The way in which they worked and interwove personal and collective meanings had strong associations with reconstructions for and "readings" of the website *A History of Aboriginal Sydney*. Once removed from the dominant presence of print, Indigenous teenagers found a way of connecting aspects of Indigenous culture with contemporary memories and communication tools. At the same time, they modeled collaborative storytelling for other students. Some non-Indigenous students decided to work in pairs in subsequent workshops, choosing popular books to present their creative reading, strongly echoing personal issues. The slow process of building a digital story using a variety of digital and analog tools enabled reflection and the construction of meaning through a personal connection with the text and a dialog with the co-authors.

4.4.1 Reader—user—creator

The snippets of digital behaviors (*Scholar, Community, Teenager*) which were observed and recorded in the three research projects that form the primary evidence for this book illustrate the practices of very different groups of people. Looking into a fuller pattern of behaviors, what emerges is not a picture, but rather an animation with numerous transitions and transformations. A clear delineation of practices, named and defined in relation to print culture, is often limited or redundant. Old habits, new ways of doing well-known activities, and new practices are coming together to shape online behaviors.

Transliterate reading emerges as the practice of reading across a range of texts when the reader seamlessly switches between different platforms, modalities, types of reading, and genres. Reading is part of a range of netchaining activities, such as searching, watching, and communicating, guided by a personal interest and context. Transliterate reading is based on abilities to search effectively, read across resources, handle files in different formats, and have a trained eye and brain to establish connections. The lines between reading, using, and creating are often blurry, but a transliterate reader demonstrates an ability to adjust reading and incorporate it in other activities. Transliterate reading does not replace or supersede traditional forms of focused and deep reading of a single text. Transliterate reading, however, extends the range of reading skills and situations when reading comprehension is required.

Netchaining emerges as a key capability in "reading across." Any number of reading practices can be part of netchaining—from in-depth reading when a useful reference is found at the bottom of the text or an argument is followed in a text, to search and skim-reading for particular information, to scan-reading for information about the author of the newly found source. The authorial voice presenting an argument or a story is replaced by the reader's/user's/creator's idea, which guides netchaining. The scholar switches between a whole range of activities and different levels of reading following the development of a guiding question. Many users of *A History of Aboriginal Sydney* said they stumbled across the site accidentally and then stayed there to explore stories related to their families and communities. Names of people, places, and events are their guiding ideas as they skim read or carefully read search results, and explore films and images. The spiral of searching—reading—watching unfolds around personal connections.

Ongoing searching and probing into the wealth of online information, which often requires a significant ability to process information quickly and make decisions about the trustworthiness of information, leads to new ways of exploring ideas. Unlike databases of the past, Internet search engines are starting to support the exploration of semiverbal ideas:

What I do love about the electronic text world is, you can get a kind of half of an idea or a hunch or a sort of tip-of-the-tongue feeling about an idea that's not quite come yet but you kind of, you might be able to form that idea and I do often do it by sort of Boolean searching, you know, by just going 'Ah, it's this, it's red and it's blue and it's sharp and it's slow, you know' [laughter] and then you think, 'Ah, give me a whole lot of other things that are like that!'

U Participant 6/2

It has been suggested that the focus on computers prevents immersion in electronic literature (Mangen & Kuiken, 2014). For website users, however, the computer is an enabler. A level of familiarity with this type of interface, which does not emphasize technological novelty, is possibly a contributing factor for "staying in a flow." It is, however, a personally meaningful story that maintains a sense of immersion and makes the user say, "Oh, my God, that was extraordinary! I stayed up all night looking at all these stories." It is a personally meaningful story developed as a result of deep reading that also keeps teenagers motivated through an often tedious process of searching for images they can use to illustrate their work. Drawing and making photographs and motion animations, which are sometimes technically demanding, are other techniques to bring one's reading to life as reading merges into creating.

The juxtaposition of ideas is an essential feature of moving across a range of information presented digitally. For a user of a website, understanding emerges from the juxtaposition of resources and snippets of information in search results. An academic described how reading across documents provides opportunities for creative insights:

> ... when you've got your computer going and you've got a couple of different documents open and you're cutting and pasting or you're toggling between two or three documents ... you're just feeling ideas come out of this idea, idea number one and idea number two, when they pop up against each other often completely other idea, idea number 25 will, sort of, turn up out of that.
>
> U Participant 6/2

New digital practices are emerging, but we currently do not have a clear understanding of the forms of reading happening on screen or in readers' interactions with mixed platforms, let alone how they can be captured and measured. What is becoming evident, however, is a need to recognize very different reading practices. The question is not so much whether we read better from the print page or screen, but which form of reading is most suitable for the task and text at hand. A cultivated ability to adjust and apply skills in novel ways online and offline may result in differently trained eyes, ears, hands, and brain to participate in a fully transliterate reading experience.

4.4.2 Education for transliterate reading and writing

An ability to "go with a digital flow" or stop for focused reading requires a new combination of skills and sophisticated metacognition. While there are rules and conventions developed over hundreds of years on how to present writing in a book; and education prepares young people for reading and interpreting ideas on paper; there are very few definitive rules for the construction of digital environments and almost no training for reading on screen. Academics and teenagers alike are unsure what they are expected to know about digital tools and resources. It takes a leap of faith to be open to the possibilities of and acknowledge "idea number 25" when it appears.

Instead of focusing on traditional reading and writing, transliteracy points toward the possibility of shedding a broader light on literacy. Engaging with one aspect of learning may become a conduit for another. For example, Student T. commented on how she discovered an interest in reading and writing through digital storytelling:

> I never would have thought I could do things like this because I'm not a very good person at writing or reading much. And this sort of helped me. Now I read a lot more and that's basically what I liked about iTell...I always thought reading was really boring, but now it's opened my eyes that it's not and it'll help me with my spelling as well because I'll learn new words and stuff so that should be good.

The end of year school report after iTell is the only one during her high school years which mentions T.'s notable engagement with texts studied in English classes. Three years after the quoted interview, I asked the student how her newly discovered interest progressed. She explained how her initial interest lasted for at least several months. She had not become an avid reader, but she did not find reading boring anymore. However, a temporary change in reading interest and habits as well as a shift in attitude provides room for the consideration of possibilities for engaging students in learning. The authors of *Hanging Out, Messing Around, and Geeking Out: Kids Living and Learning with New Media* (2010) observe that many initially exciting experiences with media and alternative forms of learning do not in themselves lead to long-lasting interests, but they provide knowledge and skills as stepping stones to deeper engagement with their environment and new areas of interest. Student interests may also translate to enhanced reading ability as they engage with a range of texts.

An argument for developing critical thinking by reading across texts was strongly promoted by Gainer and Lapp (2010). Although they did not refer to transliteracy, their book *Literacy Remix: Bridging Adolescents' In and Out-of-School Literacies* raises pertinent questions and provides examples for the introduction of transliteracy into the classroom. The authors argue:

> *Just as it did in previous time periods, reading instruction needs to change with the new demands faced by citizens. In an information age, critical literacy involving reading and writing in multiple modes is imperative. The following examples from Ms.Woollven and Robert Cheshire's 12th-grade English-social studies integrated classroom illustrate the notion that reading well in our present society involves remixing old and new literacies technologies in multiple and multimodal ways across the curriculum.*
>
> *Gainer and Lapp, 2010, p. 59*

The authors provide examples of teaching English and social studies as part of a joint research project in which students communicated their findings in a range of forms and genres for different audiences. Their argument for widening our understanding of what constitutes writing is supported by examples of a variety of multimodal written expressions.

Digital storytelling is a good example of a genre and approach to developing transliteracy, which could be used in different settings to promote transliterate reading and writing.

Digital storytelling: an approach to putting transliteracy into action

Based on Sukovic (2014)

Digital storytelling (DS) is a useful example of how transliteracy can be applied in classrooms from kindergarten to university and in situations of informal learning. Brídigo-Corachán and Gregori-Signes (2014) present a wide range of contexts in which DS has been used. Institutions, including libraries and community groups, utilize DS to record memories of a community, as was the case in the project *Capture Wales* (BBC, s.a.), and to aid

(Continued)

(cont'd)

reflection in the treatment of people recovering from trauma and adverse life events. Educational institutions use DS to engage with learners and tap into multiple intelligences and literacies (Ohler, 2008; Frazel, 2010). Opperman (2008, p. 178) observed that DS has the capacity to engage students in learning about complex ideas: "The format of the digital story allows the compression of complex ideas through the use of multiple media... For students, digital stories have proven to be a powerful medium to express their voice with intellectual depth in a form other than writing." Storytelling and emotional engagement create a learning space for students to develop a personal connection with complex theories (Benmayor, 2008; Coventry, 2008; Opperman, 2008). As a pedagogical tool, DS "brings the creator/student and the viewer together in a dialogue around the nature of representation, meaning, and authority embedded in imagery and narrative" (Fletcher and Cambre, 2009, p. 115). According to Coventry (2008), the use of multiple modalities and less familiar forms of communication through multimedia is likely to enhance learning.

DS can be used successfully to meet educational standards (Ohler, 2008; Frazel, 2010), and to make writing composition more visible, while enriching student experience with writing (Opperman, 2008). In the project Reflect 2.0, students reported that multimedia helped them to be reflective and they appreciated the opportunity to be creative (Sandars, 2009). Their tutors noted that the DS enhanced reflective learning for students who did not have a preference for writing.

DS has been described as a powerful educational tool to build confidence and establish a sense of a community and collaboration (Benmayor, 2008; Leon, 2008). Gregori-Signes (2008) discusses the usefulness of DS in a languages classroom setting, pointing out that it helps students to make themselves heard.

Traditional forms of assessment and assessed skills need to be revised. Online reading comprehension usually appears as part of research and problem solving, but the abilities to read and evaluate search result, and produce media genres are not typically assessed at school (Leu et al., 2013). Coiro (2009) demonstrated a difference in print and online reading comprehension, showing that they tap into different skills, and stressed that assessment must take this into account. Achievements assessment in project-based and cross-curricular learning provides experiences and methods to be used in conjunction with the transliteracy framework.

Conversations about transliteracy are part of broader discussions about learning and knowledge production for this century, often in contradiction to traditions. Teachers have had the unsettling feeling that they are constantly being asked for more, with many requirements clashing on operational and philosophical levels.

The answer from a transliteracy perspective lies in reconfiguring the existing educational field to allow more purposeful explorations. The area for transliteracy could be perceived as large as knowledge itself, but teachers and librarians already know how to guide learners through the knowledge field. A more difficult question concerns the removal of a common obstacle course, consisting of many requirements that do not serve student learning, to create space for exploration. Mapping what we do in the classroom and what we want to do with learning is a practical start. The use of transliteracy palettes can provide tools to encourage transliteracy to develop in many different directions, bound by the context and learners' needs. A key role of educators is to support and guide new investigations as they emerge. It is important to remember, however, that investigations and guidance can both appear in many forms. As the shifting sense of authority and leadership emerges in the society and the classroom alike, it becomes acceptable and even expected that different people may become guides during the learning process. The educator is then a teacher and learner in a thriving learning community.

4.5 Summary

This chapter started with considerations of aids and challenges to transliteracy. They revolve around two main issues: underpinning structures (such as suitable technology, access to information, time, and space) and transliteracy capabilities, particularly in relation to skills, traditions, professional development, and collaboration.

The rest of the chapter considered transliteracy and learning. Transliteracy palettes were presented as a tool for the implementation of transliteracy in teaching and learning. A transliteracy palette consists of an information and a form palette. Mixing them in as many combinations as possible in a range of contexts is proposed as a way of developing skills for transliterate "movement across." Curriculum mapping was proposed as a way of ensuring that transliteracy is embedded in classroom practice.

Pedagogies suitable for the development of transliteracy are those which enable exploration, student-based learning, and boundary-crossing. Particular attention was given to reading and writing in interaction with different technologies. Findings from the literature and transliteracy study point toward a gap in our understanding of how different technologies support existing forms of reading and writing and, especially, of emerging practices. Approaches to the development of transliterate reading and writing were considered.

References

ACRL, 2000. Information Literacy Competency Standards for Higher Education. Association of College and Research Libraries, Chicago, IL.
ACRL, 2016. Framework for Information Literacy for Higher Education. Association of College and Research Libraries, Chicago, IL.

ASCD, 2006. Getting Results with Curriculum Mapping: Facilitator's Guide. Association for Supervision and Curriculum Development, Alexandria, VA.

Australia Council for the Arts, 2014. Arts in daily life: Australian participation in the art. Australia Council for the Arts.

Baron, N.S., 2015. Words Onscreen: the Fate of Reading in a Digital World. Oxford University Press, Oxford.

BBC, s.a. Capture Wales. BBC. Available from: http://www.bbc.co.uk/wales/audiovideo/sites/galleries/pages/capturewales.shtml (accessed 24.05.16.).

Benmayor, R., 2008. Digital storytelling as a signature pedagogy for the new humanities. Arts Human. Higher Educ. 7, 188−204.

Bowen, J.L., 2014. Emotion in organizations: resources for business educators. J. Manage. Educ. 38, 114−142.

Brídigo-Corachán, A.M., Gregori-Signes, C., 2014. Digital storytellin and its expansion across educational contexts. In: Gregori-Signes, C., Brídigo-Corachán, A.M. (Eds.), Appraising Digital Storytelling Across Educational Contexts. Publicacions De La Universitat De València.

Bruce, C., Edwards, S., Lupton, M., 2006. Six frames for information literacy education: a conceptual framework for interpreting the relationships between theory and practice. Italics: Innov. Teach. Learn. Inform. Comput. Sci., 5.

Buchanan, H., Kavanagh Webb, K., Harris Houk, A., Tingelstad, C., 2015. Curriculum mapping in academic libraries. New Rev. Acad. Librar. 21, 94−111.

Bui, D.C., Myerson, J., Hale, S., 2013. Note-taking with computers: exploring alternative strategies for improved recall. J. Educ. Psychol. 105, 299−309.

Bundy, A. (Ed.), 2004. Australia and New Zealand Information Literacy Framework. Australian and New Zealand Institute for Information Literacy, Adelaide.

Bush, G., 2012. The transliterate learner. School Library Monthly 5−9, Sep/Oct.

Cazden, C., Cope, B., Fairclough, N., Gee, J., Kalantzis, M., Kress, G., et al., 1996. A pedagogy for multiliteracies: designing social futures. Harvard Educ. Rev. 66, 60−92.

Chen, D.-W., Catrambone, R., 2015. Paper vs. screen: effects on reading comprehension, metacognition, and reader behavior. Proceedings of the Human Factors and Ergonomics Society 59th Annual Meeting. 59, 332−336.

Chen, G., Cheng, W., Chang, T.-W., Zheng, X., Huang, R., 2014. A comparison of reading comprehension across paper, computer screens, and tablets: does tablet familiarity matter? J. Comput. Educ. 1, 213−225.

Coiro, J., 2009. Rethinking online reading assessment. Edu. Leadership. 66, 59−63.

Cooper, N., Lockyer, L., Brown, I., 2013. Developing multiliteracies in a technology-mediated environment. Educ. Media Int. 50, 93−107.

Coventry, M., 2008. Engaging gender: student application of theory throught digital storytelling. Arts Human. Higher Educ. 7, 205−218.

Cropley, A., 2001. Creativity in Education & Learning a Guide for Teachers and Educators. Kogan Page, London.

Csikszentmihalyi, M., 1988. Society, culture and person: a systems view of creativity. In: Sternberg, R.J. (Ed.), The Nature of Creativity: Contemporary Psychological Perspectives. Cambridge University Press, Cambridge.

Dalgleish, T., 2002. Information processing approaches to emotion. In: Davidson, R.J. (Ed.), Handbook of Affective Sciences. Oxford University Press, Cary, NC.

Damasio, A.R., 2000a. Descartes' Error: Emotion, Reason, and the Human Brain. Quill, New York.

Damasio, A.R., 2000b. The Feeling of What Happens : Body, Emotion and the Making of Consciousness. Vintage, London.

Farinosi, M., Lim, C., Roll, J., 2016. Book or screen, pen or keyboard? A cross-cultural sociological analysis of writing and reading habits basing on Germany, Italy and the UK. Telemat. Inform. 33, 410–421.

Fletcher, C., Cambre, C., 2009. Digital storytelling and implicated scholarship in the classroom. J. Canadian Stud. 43, 109–130.

Fortunati, L., Vincent, J., 2014. Sociological insights on the comparison of writing/reading on paper with writing/reading digitally. Telemat. Inform. 31, 39–51.

Foster, A., 2004. A nonlinear model of information-seeking behavior. J. Am. Soc. Inform. Sci. Technol. 55, 228–237.

Frazel, M., 2010. Digital Storytelling: Guide for Educators. International Society for Technology in Education, Eugene, Oregon.

Gainer, J., Lapp, D., 2010. Literacy Remix: Bridging Adolescents' In and Out of School Literacies. International Reading Association, Newark, DE.

Gregori-Signes, C., 2008. Integrating the old and the new: digital storytelling in the EFL language classroom. GRETA J. 16, 43–49.

Halinen, I., 2016. General aspects of basic education curriculum reform in Finland. Finnish National Board of Education.

Hanging Out, Messing Around, and Geeking Out: Kids Living and Learning with New Media, 2010. MIT Press, Cambridge, MA.

Hargittai, E., 2010. Digital na(t)ives? Variation in Internet skills in uses among members of the "Net generation". Sociol. Inquiry. 80, 92–113.

Hillesund, T., 2010. Digital reading spaces: How expert readers handle books, the Web and electronic paper. First Monday15.

Hobbs, R., 2011. Digital and Media Literacy: Connecting Culture and Classroom. Corwin Press, Thousand Oaks, CA.

Ito, M., Gutiérrez, K., Livingstone, S., Penuel, B., Rhodes, J., Salen, K., et al., 2013. Connected Learning: an Agenda for Research and Design. Digital Media and Learning Research Hub, Irvine, CA.

Jacobs, H.H. (Ed.), 2004. Getting Results with Curriculum Mapping. Association for Supervision and Curriculum Development, Alexandria, VA.

Kaluzniacky, E., 2004. Managing Psychological Factors in Information Systems Work : an Orientation to Emotional Intelligence. Information Science Pub, Hershey, PA; London.

Lacewing, M., 2004. Emotion and cognition: recent developments and therapeutic practice. Philos. Psychiatr. Psychol. 11, 175–186.

Lea, M.R., Jones, S., 2011. Digital literacies in higher education: exploring textual and technological practices. Stud. Higher Educ. 36, 377–393.

Lehmans, A., Cordier, A., 2014. Transliteracy and knowledge formats. In: Kurbanoglu, S., Spiranec, S., Grassian, E., Mizrachi, D., Catts, R. (Eds.), Information Literacy: Lifelong Learning and Digital Citizenship in the 21st Century; Second European Conference, ECIL 2014. Springer, Dubrovnik, Croatia.

Lehmans, A., Mazurier, V., 2015. Transfer, transformation, transition: what the school librarian can do in transliteracy, the French context. In: Das, L., Brand-Gruwel, S., Kok, K., Walhout, J. (Eds.), The School Library Rocks: Living it, Learning it, Loving it, 44th International Association of School Librarianship International Conference, Incorporating the 19th International Forum on Research in School Librarianship. International Association of School Librarianship, Maastricht, Netherlands.

Leon, S.M., 2008. Slowing down, talking back, and moving forward: some reflections on digital storytelling in the humanities curriculum. Arts Human. Higher Educ. 7, 220–223.

Leu, D.J., Forzani, E., Burlingame, C., Kulikowich, J.M., Sedransk, N., Coiro, J., et al., 2013. The new literacies of online research and comprehension: assessing and preparing students for the 21st century with Common Core State Standards. In: Neumann, S.B., Gambrell, L.B. (Eds.), Quality Reading Instruction in the Age of Common Core Standards. International Reading Association, Newark.

Lupton, M., 2008. Information Literacy and Learning. Auslib Press, Adelaide.

Mangen, A., Kuiken, D., 2014. Lost in an iPad: narrative engagement on paper and tablet. Sci. Study Lit. 4, 150–177.

Margolin, S.J., Driscoll, C., Toland, M.J., Kegler, J.L., 2013. E-readers, computer screens, or paper: does reading comprehension change across media platforms? Appl. Cognit. Psychol. 27, 512–519.

Megwalu, A., 2014. Transliteracy: a holistic and purposeful learning. Ref. Librar. 55, 381–384.

Merga, M.K., 2014. Are teenagers really keen digital readers?: Adolescent engagement in ebook reading and the relevance of paper books today. English Australia. 49, 27–37.

Mueller, P.A., Oppenheimer, D.M., 2014. The pen is mightier than the keyboard: advantages of longhand over laptop note taking. Psychol. Sci. 25, 1159–1168.

Nahl, D., Bilal, D. (Eds.), 2007. Information and Emotion: the Emergent Affective Paradigm in Information Behaviour Research and Theory. Information Today, Medford, NJ.

Ohler, J., 2008. Digital Storytelling in the Classroom: New Media Pathways to Literacy, Learning, and Creativity. Corwin, Thousand Oaks.

Oliver, B., Ferns, S., Whelan, B., Lilly, L., 2010. Mapping the curriculum for quality enhancement: refining a tool and processes for the purpose of curriculum renewal. Quality in Uncertain Times, Australian Quality Forum. Australian Universities Quality Agency, Gold Coast, Australia.

Opperman, M., 2008. Digital storytelling and American studies: critical trajectories from the emotional to the epistemological. Arts Human. Higher Educ. 7, 171–186.

Pang, M.F., Marton, F., 2013. Interaction between the learners' initial grasp of the object of learning and the learning resource afforded. Instruct. Sci. 41, 1065–1082.

Picton, I., 2014. The Impact of ebooks on the Reading Motivation and Reading Skills of Children and Young People: a Rapid Literature Review. National Literacy Trust, London.

Rainie, L., Perrin, A., 2015. Slightly Fewer Americans Are Reading Print Books, New Survey Finds. Pew Research Center.

Rainie, L., Zickuhr, K., Purcell, K., Madden, M., Brenner, J., 2012. The Rise of e-reading. Pew Research Center's Internet & American Life Project, Washington.

Robinson, K., 2011. Out of our Minds: Learning to be Creative. Capstone, Oxford.

Robinson, M.D., Watkins, E.R., Harmon-Jones, E., 2013. Handbook of Cognition and Emotion. Guilford Publications, New York.

Roy Morgan Research, 2014, July 21. Reading between the lines: Books and digital not so incompatible.

Roy Morgan Research, 2016, May 10. Australia's reading habits: the good (and not-so-good) news.

Sahlberg, P., 2015. Finland's school reforms won't scrap subjects altogether. The Conversation.

Sandars, J., 2009. Reflect 2.0: Using digital storytelling to develop reflective learning by the use of Next Generation Technologies and practices. University of Leeds.

Scherer, K.R., 2002. Introduction: cognitive components of emotion. In: Davidson, R.J. (Ed.), Handbook of Affective Sciences. Oxford University Press, Cary, NC.

Spencer, D., Riddle, M., Knewstubb, B., 2012. Curriculum mapping to embed graduate capabilities. Higher Educ. Res. Dev. 31, 217–231.

Stoop, J., Kreutzer, P., Kircz, J., 2013. Reading and learning from screens versus print: a study in changing habits. New Librar. World. 114, 284–300.

Sukovic, S., 2014. iTell: transliteracy and digital storytelling. Austral. Acad. Res. Librar. 45, 205–229.

Sukovic, S., 2015. Transliterate reading. Scholar. Res. Commun.6.

Taipale, S., 2014. The affordances of reading/writing on paper and digitally in Finland. Telemat. Informat. 31, 532–542.

Taipale, S., 2015. Bodily dimensions of reading and writing practices on paper and digitally. Telemat. Informat. 32, 766–775.

The Center for International Scholarship in School Libraries, 2016. Guided Inquiry. Rutgers, the State University of New Jersey. Available from: http://cissl.rutgers.edu/joomla-license/guided-inquiry (accessed 15.06.16.).

The New South Wales Department of Education and Training, 2007. Information skills in the school: engaging learners in constructing knowledge. In: School Libraries and Information Literacy Unit, C. K. D. (ed.).

Thomas, S., 2013. Making a space: transliteracy and creativity. Digital Creat. 24, 182–190.

Vandenhoek, T., 2013. Screen reading habits among university students. Int. J. Educ. Develop. Inform. Commun. Technol. 9, 37–47.

Wang, C.-L., 2015. Mapping or tracing? Rethinking curriculummapping in higher education. Stud. Higher Educ. 40, 1550–1559.

Weiss, R.P., 2000. Emotion and learning. Train. Develop., November, 45–48.

Willett, T.G., 2008. Current status of curriculum mapping in Canada and the UK. Med. Educ. 42, 786–793.

Zhao, Y., 2012. World class learners: educating creative and enterpreneurial students. Corwin, Thousand Oaks, CA.

Transliterate cultures

5.1 Academic cultures and transliteracy

It was established in the previous chapters that transliteracy as a practice is not new, but has emerged in the last decade as an epistemic framework to capture changes, which have been introduced or amplified by the development of digital technologies. For education and scholarly work, digital alternatives, especially in interaction with the multiplicity of digital resources, are on the rise against the dominance of print, igniting major cultural shifts. Transliterate movement across a range of information sources and technologies traverses the center of the cultural shift involving technological, cultural, and broader societal changes. In considering how transliteracy becomes a part of the change affecting academia, investigations of research practices and behaviors of scholars in the humanities provide the best starting point.

Text is fundamental to scholars in the humanities, whose work is based on studying textual records and reflecting on their nature. Jerome McGann, a humanist scholar, famously wrote: "Textual studies is ground zero of everything we do. We read, we write, we think in a textual condition. Because that is true, the new information and media technologies go to the core of our work" (McGann, 1998, p. 609). These scholars have a long tradition of engagement with text in various forms and from all periods, so they are in a position to reflect on the changes. An essential part of their work is a dialog with texts past and present, which is valuable in considering the impact of the current transition. Historical and literary studies are of particular interest as they are especially reliant on textual studies and print. In modern academia, literary studies include traditional historical, critical, and theoretical research as well as creative writing, which provides possible access to changes in creative and analytical approaches to academic work.

The potential importance of investigating the interactions of humanists with texts in digital format has been recognized by a number of authors. Belkin wrote about plans to investigate these interactions: "By studying humanists, we assume that we will observe behaviors which may not have been observed in studies of scientists, and we will therefore be able to extend our general knowledge of human interactions with text substantially" (Belkin, 1994, p. 483).

In the first part of this chapter, we will consider what interactions with the multiplicity of resources mean for the construction of knowledge, especially in the humanities, in which academic authority is based on authentic sources. Changes in the way academics conduct research and evaluate their work are closely related to interactions with digital technologies as well as broader societal changes, particularly those concerning scholarly traditions and positions of authority. Some of these issues were considered in my previous work in relation to citation of electronic

Transliteracy in Complex Information Environments. DOI: http://dx.doi.org/10.1016/B978-0-08-100875-1.00005-4

sources (Sukovic, 2009) and construction of environments for information discovery in ambiguous zones of research (Sukovic, 2008). Parts of the two articles have been used in this chapter.

5.1.1 Academic authority and authenticity of multiple sources

It is to have a compulsive, repetitive, and nostalgic desire for the archive, an irrepressible desire to return to the origin, a homesickness, a nostalgia for the return to the most archaic place of absolute commencement.

Derrida

Academic authority is the basis of an academic career in which the establishment of cognitive authority depends on the selection of authentic information sources. Two major barriers to users' access to information identified by Buckland (1991) are cognitive access and acceptability. Cognitive access means that the recipient has "sufficient expertise to understand or, at least, misunderstand the information," and acceptability means that "[t]he recipient must be willing to accept the information, believing it to be true and not rejecting it as awkward" (Buckland, 1991, p. 113). The latter is particularly important in the context of scholarly information use.

Acceptability of information can be considered in terms of cognitive authority, defined as "influence on one's thoughts that one would consciously recognize as proper" (Wilson, 1983, p. 15). The reliance on authoritative information sources, particularly trustworthy primary data, is critical in establishing a scholar's cognitive authority. A scholar's belief that textual materials that constitute primary data are trustworthy is based on her or his judgment that:

1. text as a document is trustworthy because its origins can be clearly established, and the characteristics of representation can be explained and understood. It is possible to answer with confidence questions such as "Does this text represent what it claims to represent?" and "How does it represent it?"

2. the authority of textual content can be established. Questions about the content, such as "Who wrote the text?," "For what purposes?," "In what context?" can be either answered or understood in the context of textual production.

The two aspects are connected, but they are not the same. A digitized document may be a trustworthy representation of a print edition, but the selection of an edition for digitization may be problematic, or editorial processes of selection and context-building may be questionable. Burnett and McKinley (1998, pp. 287–288) suggested that the perception of cognitive authority might be affected by the medium through which a document is received. More verifiable media, such as print, are perceived to have more cognitive authority, but in situations when currency was important, databases would have more authority than books. Participant 14/1 talked about investigating hard copies of electronic documents to establish the full context in which they were used because electronic sources may promote one perspective only. In this case, an e-text was viewed as a trustworthy document, but a questionable selection process made it difficult for a researcher to establish the meaning of the document. A detailed explanation of representation processes is critical for establishing the trustworthiness of an electronic document. A number of study participants talked about verifying electronic sources against hard copies when they were available. For some of them, evaluation of all the characteristics of these documents would help in identifying the most reliable source. The closeness to the original, as well as trust in established institutions and their publishing processes, are important factors in judging trustworthiness.

The trustworthiness of electronic documents may be more difficult to establish, but often they are a better source of information than the original when they are presented by reliable authorities. Electronic documents provide minute details which are not accessible to most people, as well as a wealth of contextual information and documentation about their provenance. Many scholarly electronic projects present information from and about marginalized groups of people which does not exist in print sources.

However, the authenticity and authority of a text are often perceived in the context of scholars' quest for its origin, described by Derrida as "archive fever":

> The trouble de l'archive stems from a mal d'archive. We are en mal d'archive: in need of archives. Listening to the French idiom, and in it the attribute en mal de, to be en mal d'archive can mean something else than to suffer from a sickness, from a trouble or from what the noun mal might name. It is to burn with a passion. It is never to rest, interminably, from searching for the archive right where it slips away. ... It is to have a compulsive, repetitive, and nostalgic desire for the archive, an irrepressible desire to return to the origin, a homesickness, a nostalgia for the return to the most archaic place of absolute commencement.
>
> Derrida, 1996, p. 91

As Derrida argued, the archive is the place where things *commence* and also the place "where men and gods *command, there* where authority, social order are exercised" (Derrida, 1996, p. 1). An uneasy fit of the place of commencement and the place of commandment becomes evident in considering the meaning of authenticity, particularly in the electronic environment. An important question concerns who presented not only an electronic copy but also the "real thing," and how these were presented. The official authority of the author, publisher, or a curating institution is often important in establishing the trustworthiness of information, but it does not necessarily guarantee authenticity. As Haraway pointed out, representation is rarely a reproduction. Haraway used an example of the jaguar and the fetus, which cannot represent themselves: "Both the jaguar and the fetus are carved out of one collective entity and relocated in another, where they are reconstituted as objects of a particular kind—as the ground of a representational practice that *forever* authorizes the ventriloquist. Tutelage will be eternal" (Haraway, 1992, p. 312). When Haraway questioned the right of a scientist to represent "the nature," she questioned representation authorities. The question is particularly acute in the framework of electronic environments, in which a variety of representations with different origins keeps open questions of who represented something, in what way and for what purposes. The understanding of trustworthiness of representation that arises from Haraway's perspective concerns the reliability of reproduction as much as ideologically charged contexts of representation.

Many reputable electronic projects represent the knowledge of marginalized groups whose documents are usually absent from institutional archives. In these situations, electronic records provide the most authentic accessible information. However, the act of representation without a full scholarly apparatus and the backing of a disciplinary tradition leaves these records in a limbo. Authentic information needs to be recognized and connected in a meaningful argument by an authoritative mind. When Participant 2/2 explained how she felt removed from the search results produced by a search engine and demonstrated justified pride in finding the best ways to retrieve information, she implicitly alluded to the concept of scholarly work in which a humanist looks at a range of information and, with the help of a trained eye and a sharp mind, recognizes relevant pieces, which will be put together in an individually constructed argument, demonstrating the scholar's ingenuity and cognitive authority. Peter Read explained the view of his colleagues about his decision to present authentic records of Indigenous history online:

> When I did my seminar on what I was doing, I got a good deal of approbation from young PhD scholars, but not much from the senior staff who said, "What are you doing this for?" And I said, "Well, actually, what are we supposed to do as historians? Get all the information we can and communicate to a wide audience. That's what I am doing." It wasn't quite an acceptable explanation because, after all, there is that personal input—mine—of course there is, but not as much as if you are writing something which you carefully nurtured and thought of every phrase yourself, which is what one does or tries to do as a writer.
>
> HoAS, Peter Read

Historical records presented unfiltered "to an historian's opinion. . . right from the horse's mouth" (HoAS, Julie Janson) are highly authentic. However, they appear as a claim of truth among the multiplicity of truths and that makes an uneasy fit with a sense of academic authority. Lyotard thought that power relations had a strong influence on knowledge claims. The truth and credibility were relative and dependent on consensus which, in turn, depended on the truth of statements supporting the claims:

> No money, no proof—and that means no verification of statements and no truth. The games of scientific language become the games of the rich, in which whoever is wealthiest has the best chance of being right. An equation between wealth, efficiency, and truth is thus established.
>
> Lyotard, 1984, p. 45

Despite dominant power relationships associated with claims to knowledge and truth, Foucault (1980, p. 81) found "insurrection of subjugated knowledges." They appeared as buried and disguised historical content and as "a whole set of knowledges that have been disqualified as inadequate to their task or insufficiently elaborated: naive knowledges, located low down on the hierarchy, beneath the required level of cognition or scientificity" (Foucault, 1980, p. 82). Foucault argued that critical discourses in the previous "fifteen years have in effect discovered their essential force in this association between the buried knowledges of erudition and those disqualified from the hierarchy of knowledges and sciences" (p. 82). He named this union *genealogy* and saw it as anti-sciences, "opposed primarily not to the contents, methods or concepts of a science, but to the effects of the centralising powers which are linked to the institution and functioning of an organised scientific discourse within a society such as ours" (p. 84). Genealogy is related to Deleuze and Guattari's rhizomatic systems:

> *It is based on a reactivation of local knowledges—of minor knowledges, as Deleuze might call them—in opposition to the scientific hierarchisation of knowledges and the effects intrinsic to their power: this, then, is the project of these disordered and fragmentary genealogies.*
>
> *Foucault, 1980, p. 85*

Textual tradition, the power of knowledge institutions, and suppressed knowledges all come into play in constructing knowledge on the basis of analog and digital resources of different provenance. The concept of intertextuality is particularly relevant for this discussion because hypertextuality and multimedia emphasize and develop textual connections and polysemy, which are the central ideas of intertextuality. Nelson summarized the role of intertextuality in contemporary thought and in relation to hypertextuality:

> *Now poststructuralism [and, with it, the concept of intertextuality] has been appropriated in various disciplines from history to psychology, from education to computer science. In computer science, for instance, some have synthesized intertextuality with the theoretical aspects of hypertext. For instance, George Landow [1992] has argued that hypertext is the 'literal embodiment' of intertextuality.*
>
> *Nelson, 2001, p. 391*

Visual aspects of online content contribute to making connections explicit. Although we were always passing the text from one person to another, which "is the literal meaning of the word 'tradition'," Bolter notes that we "are now using the computer to simplify the technology of intertextuality so much that we seem to be refashioning the idea of tradition itself" (Bolter, 2001, p. 179).

An overwhelming sense of everything that is "out there," connected in ways that makes any institutional organization of knowledge temporary and conditional, is closely related to Kristeva's concepts of ambivalence and carnival. Kristeva explained Bakhtin's literary theory in which "any text is constructed as a mosaic of quotations; any text is the absorption and transformation of another. The notion of *intertextuality* replaces that of intersubjectivity, and poetic language is read as at least *double*" (Kristeva, 1980, p. 66). This leads to the concept of ambivalence, which is related to the polysemy of poetic language. Literary semiotics requires a

0−2, instead of a 0−1 interval. "The only discourse integrally to achieve the 0−2 poetic logic is that of the carnival. By adopting a dream logic, it transgresses rules of linguistic code and social morality as well" (p. 70). It means obeying another law. In Western culture, it is present "as an often misunderstood and persecuted substratum" (p. 78) noticeable in folk games, medieval theater, and prose. The polyphonic novels of Rabelais, Swift, Dostoevsky, Joyce, Proust, and Kafka, for example, have a carnivalesque structure, explained Kristeva. Connections among items of online content produced by anyone regardless of, and sometimes despite, the rules that govern the society have a carnivalesque structure.

Kristeva discussed Menippean discourse as a particular aspect of textual dialog, which emphasizes "the text as social activity" (Kristeva, 1980, p. 82). The tradition of Menippean discourse includes stories about adventures in the underworld, and it "is both comic and tragic, or rather, it is *serious* in the same sense as is the carnivalesque; through the status of its words, it is politically and socially disturbing" (p. 82). Menippean discourse "is an all-inclusive genre, put together as a pavement of citations" (p. 83) and characterized by multistylism and multitonality.

The coexistence of a variety of texts with different origins, polysemy of connected texts, visual images, and multimedia—all form a ground for the growth of intertextuality and carnivalesque structures. Shifting and instability are part of the online dynamics, which takes mutability and connectedness, inherited with the textual tradition, as its organizational principle.

5.1.2   Research in flux

And academia can't handle people in the traditional humanities to do it digitally. You can't assess them. And it's the problem that the humanities have to solve. And haven't yet. And it keeps people in one particular direction.

HoAS, Peter Read

The judgment of the authority of digital resources and attitudes to the use of a variety of information from different sources happens in the context of the changing attitude to authority in general. Participant 5/2 commented that people were not interested in institutions and their long traditions any more, but how something related to their own life. Participant 13/1 said that people were no longer "trustful of single authoritative disposition, single authoritative discourse, they want to be able to cross-reference, cross-check, find a secondary opinion, etc. etc., and come to their own belief rather than just accept an authorized view."

The fact that some participants perceived interactions with a wide range of sources as an influence on their academic writing was discussed earlier. The way of developing an argument has been changing from dealing with firm propositions to representing the complexity of possible views and approaches. The changes in the way people research and want to present their arguments promote the use of digital resources, while some traditional practices tend to inhibit their use. The participants commented on connections between changing research approaches and the engagement with digital texts in relation to research topics and resources; and disciplines, genres, and publishing.

5.1.2.1 Research topics and sources

In the dynamic field, traditional sources of information do not have the same exclusive value as they used to, because new sources of information have become relevant as well: "We find out about things on CNN, off the web sites, out of blogs, just think of how important blogs have been during the Iraq war, and journalists and magazine staff writers can actually produce really significant material" (U Participant 5/2). A quickly articulated response to some of these materials can be valuable for an understanding of current events.

Online textual materials have contributed to the investigation of contemporary topics. I asked Participant 5/2 what had changed in academic practice, considering that some important events were happening during the 20th century as well and people knew about them. Participant 5/2 responded: "It was just accepted that the kind of sober, reflective study would come later. And also, academics didn't work so much on really contemporary material."

The choices of research topics and information sources are interlinked. Online resources have become part of a negotiation between new academic interests and demands, on one hand, and the tradition, on the other. Work on contemporary topics was not a traditional practice in historical research, but an increasing number of scholars nowadays want to research current phenomena. Some participants commented that it had become common that academics gather at conferences and seminars to reflect on recently published books, contemporary events, and topics from popular culture. The described reasons were twofold. First, the research of contemporary topics was faster, so it has become necessary to satisfy job demands and provide output required for career advancement. Secondly, it is important to historicize current issues and events. Participant 14/1 talked about certain phenomena that can be observed on websites and the need to document their occurrences and make a comment based on historical criticism. Participant 5/2 also discussed a need to make an academic comment based on researching current events, but she thought that more traditional historians did not accept this sort of research.

Digital resources provide material for researching contemporary issues, but they are often dismissed with other nontraditional sources, such as newspaper articles and films, as inappropriate for academic research. Participant 5/2 commented on "dressing up" research on contemporary topics to make it more acceptable to traditional colleagues. An accepted disciplinary theory and references are the main tools used for "dressing up," as well as demonstrating "that things that used to be thought of as ephemeral or transient can now have greater importance for people." The main purpose of "dressing up" is to connect the research with "an existing discourse. That's important. To convince those in power in the discourse" (U Participant 5/2). When asked about the role of digital texts in the shift to contemporary topics, the researcher answered that websites were the best way to access alternative communities and their documentation. Participant 5/2 saw changes in the selection of research topics and sources of information as signs of a collapse of high into low culture, which affected academic approaches to research.

5.1.2.2 Disciplines, genres, and publishing

The emergence of new genres and new ways of dealing with different media and formats can become a ground for new disciplines to emerge. The emergence of peer networks formulates a sense of an emerging discipline:

> *English departments would sometimes be the last sort of refuge for people who are starting to get interested in other forms of study like film studies [. . .]. So it kind of makes sense that someone who's starting to bring their text values to more interactive online spaces like the Internet, they would see the work become more like multimedia art or something like that. It's just that when you're one of the first ones to do it, you're not aware that that's what's happened until you start getting various kinds of feedback, . . . emerging network of contacts you realise, oh, it's no longer English space, it's now something else.*
>
> *U Participant 15/1*

In the emerging field, the researcher formed his work without considering possible views of existing disciplinary authorities: "In other words, I'm not trying to write with an audience of referees in mind hoping that they will accept my argument. I'm just writing . . ." (Participant 15/1). Experimentations with digital texts seem to promote the emergence of new styles, genres, and, eventually, disciplines, which, in turn, promote the further use of digital texts.

Publication of these experiments and their evaluation are an entirely different matter. After at least a couple of decades of discussions about different ways of evaluating academic work, publication of academic books and journal articles remains the main way of asserting one's scholarly authority and promoting a career. There are differences between disciplines, universities, and countries, but "publish or perish" summarizes what dictates academic careers in the Western world. A number of participants mentioned that even academic journals are less valued if they are not published in print as well as electronically. It may be a sign of a negative attitude toward online publishing: "So I do think there's that lingering kind of prejudice amongst academics about, that online publishing in general, but I think that that's changed" (U Participant 11/1). The observation that "anybody can set up an electronic journal" (U Participant 14/1) invokes discussions about its lack of authority.

The issue of publishing relates to the use of digital sources in the sense that researchers decide to use them in their writing in a way that is suitable for the dominant forms of publishing. As discussed earlier, publishing options determine the choice of formats for the presentation of research results. Participants 16/1 and 2/2, for example, talked about writing in a traditional way because they expected to publish in a print publication. However, a publisher's interest in the inclusion of multimedia also encourages the researcher to think about different ways of including digital resources in final works. Participant 2/2 wrote a traditional academic work for print but found that the publisher wanted to relate multimedia elements to the print publication: "It was quite exciting to hear the publisher say they are interested in doing that, then I know . . . they are thinking about multimedia." Researchers noted publishers' approaches to referencing of digital sources, as well as the way they wanted to deal with multimedia in published works, as an indication of how to shape research practices.

Despite some encouraging examples, Peter Read commented that, for an Australian historian, publishing requirements are becoming even narrower than they used to be and added:

> *And academia can't handle people in the traditional humanities to do it digitally. You can't assess them. And it's the problem that the humanities have to solve. And haven't yet. And it keeps people in one particular direction ...The young scholar setting up today on the basis of the PhD, which is still set like that, the next thing is to write a big book. Some people go in different directions and certainly the academy has tried to push us all in the other direction to write papers all the time.*

Publishing a variety of outputs with different styles and multimedia is an issue in many disciplines. Apart from being difficult to assess, there is a need to convince scholars in some disciplines that multimedia can represent real scholarship (Burgess and Hamming, 2011). This situation has implications for career advancement, especially for junior scholars. It is not an accident that most active humanists and social scientists working with digital media are at the post-tenure career stage (DLF, 2004). A professor in the transliteracy study confirmed how seniority provides some freedom from career demands: "I may not write any articles at all because ... there's nowhere to be promoted to as a full professor, I have no reason to write things just for the sake of it, I have to write what I want to write" (U Participant 14/1).

Andersen (2004) discussed a complex way in which an organizational culture, and senior and junior academics, influence each other. If digital scholarship has not been rated highly, junior scholars quickly learn that it is not a good way to develop their careers. In interdependence between an individual academic and the group, individual preferences may shape organizational cultures, so academics who do not want to rely on technology in research are less likely to teach about technology, while senior scholars who are more active in digital scholarship value this sort of research in the promotion and review process. There seems to be a gap between a push from university administrations to use computers and include them in teaching, and history departments where chairs were concerned that these activities did not help junior scholars in meeting promotion criteria (Andersen and Trinkle, 2004, p. 73). The recent prominence of digital humanities and interest in digital scholarship at universities do not necessarily translate into structures to support transliterate explorations in academia.

5.1.3   Community of scholars

> *... the big guns have grown up in a different kind of scholarship and they're the ones who edit the journals and who run the big publishing houses. So another thing that's important is that you convince them that you really can do real scholarship... It's a kind of professional accreditation problem that people who work in kind of out there fields are stuck with.*
>
> *Participant 5/2*

Disciplinary traditions and academic institutions are significant factors that shape scholars' practices and attitudes. Disciplines and institutions can both be viewed in the context of Taylor's elements of information use environments, which determine how assumptions which academics make about the nature of their work are part of general academic and more specific disciplinary traditions (Taylor, 1991). The kinds and structures of problems considered to be important relate to disciplinary views, and the constraints and opportunities of typical environments in which academics operate are part of disciplinary and institutional settings. Disciplines influence not only norms and practices, but the construction of meaning as well. A dispersed, but connected "community of interpretation" constructs meanings of documents (Brown and Duguid, 1996).

Scholars in an academic field form a community that sets the standards for scholarly research and have the final say in evaluation of the work through the peer review process. A sense of the community and disciplinary rules vary among different disciplines but, regardless of the strength of community ties and different views within a discipline, scholars identify with their discipline. "The use of appropriate sources and literature, analyses, theories, and even jargon are all evaluated" (Neumann, 2001, p. 186). Physical objects have a role as strong identification signals. Shelves full of books and filing cabinets filled with paper signal "'I am a humanities scholar', and 'this is what is important to me'. ... Clearly these 'symbols' are the heart of humanities' scholars work" (Neumann, 2001, p. 138). These signposts mark knowledge domains, which usually do not shift rapidly, but rather in the process of steady evolution (Becher, 1989).

Participants' perceptions of the research culture in which they work underpinned decisions made during the research process, particularly the way in which they presented research results. The understanding of dominant disciplinary views provides a framework for considering issues of changing research traditions in which new practices play a part. Digital resources and practice contribute to and are influenced by the interplay between tradition and change, which can be observed in the perception of peers and generational change, as well as daily balance between reflective slow research and job demands.

5.1.3.1 Peers

The success of a research project is often judged by peers' reactions. Participant 14/1 said that "the only thing which would make it [research project] flop is the way historians, the profession receives what you write, what your research is." Researchers discussed and demonstrated with their choices of how to present research results that they carefully considered peers' reactions. There was an element of anxiety because of possible harsh judgments: "And for academics, there's always this anxiety around people dying to trip you up over something, that kind of anxiety academics have about competitiveness and all that stuff" (U Participant 1/2).

When asked about peers' acceptance of electronic resources, most participants initially answered that they were generally accepted and the use was supported, but further discussions revealed that the researchers were not sure what their colleagues were thinking about these resources and what they were doing with them. The perceptions of peers' attitudes were often based on clues rather than on open discussions or clear evidence. No one mentioned a formal discussion within a disciplinary group about the use of digital materials. As Participant 14/1 said, electronic resources were "something that might be discussed in the staffroom as a kind of lunchtime topic, along with plagiarism and whatever else."

The perception that traditional academic historians were opposed to the use of electronic resources was strong enough that one of the researchers wrote a book in which he avoided mentioning them in order to keep this part of the audience engaged. Omitting e-texts from the references was a way of ensuring that more conservative historians remained focused on the argument. Although the researcher believed that some of these resources used in the research were serious and authoritative, and he did not have a policy of avoiding the mention of electronic sources in published works, he did not want to cite them in this particular book:

I didn't want to leave any distracting elements whereby the sorts of people whom I want to have an argument with the book, would argue over that issue which in fact is a minor issue, I wanted to make sure that ... if they wanted an argument with the book, they had to argue with the key ideas and that I wanted to also show that these key ideas in the book could be put to them within their own protocols, if that makes sense.

U Participant 6/2

This particular book not only dealt with a controversial topic, but also was written in a way which combined the traditional historical with the literary style of writing and challenged traditional notions of an academic historical text. The researcher used electronic resources extensively during the research process and they influenced his choice of writing style. When asked if the nontraditional academic style had anything to do with the decision to exclude e-texts from the book, the researcher responded:

... I knew that I was already pushing the edges and taking risks with the style that I didn't want to lose those people, I wanted to challenge them, but keep them in the book. And ... I did think if I start to throw in sort of citations that are from a protocol that they don't agree with, it might be the way where they could just say, 'Uh, this book, I don't, I don't need to engage with it any more'.

U Participant 6/2

Peers' resistance was more a subtle feeling than an explicit pressure. Even the researcher who omitted electronic sources to make sure that more conservative colleagues stayed with the book did not find strong evidence that peers were opposed to the use of e-texts: "I'm feeling that that's the case, but I actually don't feel ... bullied by that at all" (U Participant 6/2). For this participant, the presentation of research "was a strategic question of writing in relation to authority."

Another researcher talked about "feeling uneasy" that research could be based on Internet sources:

> *But if you're writing your work, like at the moment I'm writing a kind of general synthesis and I could get a lot of the materials off the Internet, but I would feel very uneasy about presenting that to a profession which would sort of look at it and say, oh I suppose would say, 'Oh, it's all just from Internet sources'. There is a prejudice against Internet sources.*
>
> U Participant 14/1

Some researchers discussed peers' mixed responses to electronic sources. Participant 15/1 talked about different reactions to experiments based on e-texts, but a variety of responses seemed to be common in other areas of e-text use as well. When asked what colleagues thought about the researcher's experimental academic work, Participant 15/1 responded:

> *Like with everybody, I think it's mixed. There are some who don't understand it or don't see any value in it, because it doesn't really meet what they think of as the standard. Then there are many others who are interested in the experiments that are taking place and are interested in expanding the concept of . . . what it means to write an academic paper . . .*

Conflicting peers' responses were apparent in a situation when a researcher wrote an article on research based on a range of nontraditional sources, including e-texts. This was the article that had the highest number of references to e-texts found in the study of the roles of e-texts. The article also referred to other unconventional academic sources. The project had a contemporary topic for which traditional academic sources did not exist:

> *And when I wrote the [topic] article, the two referees from the journal, one of them sent back a no, saying every source in this is a newspaper or magazine article or television documentary, it's not proper academic work. And the other one said, "Cutting edge, deeply original, should be published."*
>
> U Participant 9/1

The researcher changed the article so that it excluded part of the original research to include some academic sources. This article was the first academic response to a contemporary event and, as the researcher said "It's now been cited by at least half a dozen other people who are now working on [topic]."

A positive attitude to the practice of using e-sources may depend on the field and the quality of available materials. In fields where electronic resources seemed to be accepted, originals were not readily accessible and scholars were used to working with facsimiles, transcriptions, or translations. Where the major electronic editions were prepared by highly respected experts, discussions about e-texts revolved around these editions. One senior participant thought that there was a more positive attitude toward primary than toward secondary sources in electronic formats because of the limitations of physical collections:

> *I could say that the attitude towards using primary texts online is very different*
> *from the attitude of say learning to use Web materials and do online courses.*
> *I think the attitude is quite positive as far as primary resources are concerned*
> *because most people realise that we can't be the Library of Congress. But whether*
> *a great number of people actually use primary texts online, I couldn't say.*
>
> *U Participant 11/1*

People working in relatively new departments, such as creative communication or media studies, did not seem to be affected by peers' resistance because they cited e-texts when appropriate, and they either did not discuss peers' attitudes or said that they were not concerned with negative views. Participant 15/1, for example, said he wrote "without an umpire or referee in mind."

The discussed perceptions indicated that peers' negative attitudes and uncertainty about the peers' attitudes were a factor that inhibited a full engagement with electronic sources, particularly in terms of citing them in published works. Peers' positive attitudes to the use of digital materials were only hinted at, but they were not discussed as an influence on participants' work.

5.1.3.2   Generational change

The researcher's age was repeatedly mentioned as a contributing factor that can influence the use of e-texts. Participants related the know-how of interactions with electronic sources to age. Before considering participants' views of generational differences, I need to stress that I did not observe any difference in participants' attitudes to and descriptions of interactions with e-texts based on their seniority. I did not gather information about participants' ages, but the only difference that I could note was that the participation in online forums was mentioned only by some participants who were obviously younger researchers.

Since most participants were researchers as well as teachers, they repeatedly referred to plagiarism and an inadequate use of e-texts in students' assignments in relation to the authority of electronic resources. Examples of the lack of critical evaluation in students' work were used as a way of explaining scholars' dismissive attitude to online sources:

> *So because we're not training our students in discernment in use of electronic*
> *sources, it's all getting downgraded. So you will say, we'll dismiss the whole Net*
> *on the basis of what our student—that'll be in our work, we don't really mean that,*
> *but that would be something you'd say that someone else would understand, "all*
> *that crap from the Net."*
>
> *U Participant 7/1*

The researchers did not want to be seen as similar to their young students. On the other hand, older academics needed training for effective use of e-texts, which became an obstacle in itself. There was also a perception that younger people were better suited for current job demands and the work with electronic sources, which often required fast work on more focused projects. Participant 5/2 talked about a large recently published book authored by an older academic and said: "And that maybe is something to do with being, as they say, MTV generation, that you've got a bit of a shortened attention span, maybe. I mean, obviously, I can understand writing a 300-page book but a 700-page book . . ."

Some academics discussed that academia is going through a period of transitions, which unfold with a generational change:

> . . . this school has only recently retired the last two people who didn't use a computer at all. Most of the younger people are extremely adept. I'm one of the oldest members of staff and the young members of staff are just using the stuff routinely. In many ways it would've been better to talk to them than me, I am a transitional figure.
>
> *U Participant 14/1*

Older scholars were also more likely to be in a position of power from which they would promote traditional forms of scholarship. Participant 5/2 considered a role of academic authority figures in channeling changes in research practices and the issue of academic accreditation:

> And so the big guns have grown up in a different kind of scholarship and they're the ones who edit the journals and who run the big publishing houses. So another thing that's important is that you convince them that you really can do real scholarship the way they see real scholarship, even though you are moving into risky and different material, it's still real, it's serious, you know how to use a library and do proper footnotes and all that kind of thing. So those sorts of things are important. I think that's basically it. It's a kind of professional accreditation problem that people who work in really kind of out there fields are stuck with.

Becher concluded on the basis of his research that senior scholars have a vested interest in maintaining the *status quo*. After a significant intellectual investment they have made to develop their expertise, "(a) new development which threatens seriously to undermine the value of one's existing intellectual shareholding is unlikely to be welcomed with much enthusiasm." (Becher, 1989, p. 72).

5.1.3.3 Slow research and job demands

The participants at different stages of their career commented on increasing job demands, particularly that fast research is necessary for younger academics. Participant 9/1 commented that scholars in the early and middle stages of their careers could not afford to spend a long time on a project. Electronic resources were very helpful in speeding up the research process. Effective use of time was an important reason for some researchers to use electronic sources in short spurts. However, the conditions of interactions in brief periods of available time do not promote full engagement with research. For some people, work in short spurts changes the interaction with text, which is perceived as spasmodic and stressful.

However, the use of electronic sources, including e-texts, has become a necessary part of any research career. Participants stressed job demands as an important reason for the use of electronic sources because they enabled faster research. At the same time, some of them saw a heavy workload and tasks that they did not perceive to be important as a barrier to research in general.

The speed of interactions with online resources was often mentioned as an important aspect of those interactions. Instant access to a large body of texts is a particularly important feature of the medium of e-texts, not only because it allows faster research, but it facilitates "pursuing the sort of question that just'd be so uneconomic to ask" otherwise (U Participant 6/1). Quick interactions also enable exploration of half-formed ideas, which was not possible in interactions with analog sources (U Participant 6/2). Participant 3/1 stressed that quick access to online sources made possible the browsing of dispersed collections, which were not used when research was done in traditional ways, because most projects did not have the time and money required for physical access to dispersed materials.

At the same time, research in the office aided by computer tools was described as a quick and easy way of working, but interactions with text were not deep. For Participant 1/2, the speed of interactions with electronic resources was an element that contributed to the perception that "you're getting something easily" and it did not feel right. The researcher elaborated:

> It's [research] supposed to be bloody hard and it's supposed to be all that stuff around poring away in libraries for hours and hours and hours. And apart from the shift it's the pleasure of doing that when you do get a nice quiet library and it feels wonderful to have this lovely slow research. With the Internet it always feels slightly different. Maybe it's a bit like the slow food, fast food argument. Old-style research ... it's a bit more like kind of a cooking a meal that takes all day and the Internet's more like a hamburger.
>
> *U Participant 1/2*

Relatively quick research did not feel like proper research: "I think a lot of people worry that what they're doing in using the Internet is somehow Mickey Mouse or lazy or unethical in some way" (U Participant 1/2). A number of participants stressed that there was no substitute for reading a lot, which cannot be a fast process. Even a slow process of searching hard copies has its advantages because it allows reflection and fosters a deeper understanding of the problem. As Participant 8/1 explained, "you can ask a question, get an answer in ten minutes, what might take you in earlier days a year to get through. And the process of going through it, the question develops and deepens." This researcher found that the process of creating a database was similar to the old style of research, when a slow process allowed reflection, but then quick interactions generated new ways of exploring research questions. The researcher found the process of constructing a database too time-consuming to repeat it in other projects, but found the whole experience valuable and suggested that novice researchers would benefit from experiencing a long process of research. He compared different research processes to working with clay, by either using a mold or doing everything by hand.

Participant 9/1 said that fast research was considered shallow and not respected by peers, which is difficult to reconcile with academics' normal way of working nowadays. The researcher thought that old skills and old ways of working could not be managed while working 50 hours a week on a range of academic duties:

> If you took ten years to produce a book, even if it were a masterpiece, you would probably get sacked. Well, it's difficult to get sacked but, you know ... that kind of idea about being immersed in scholarship and being able to take time to think about what it is really that you think about your subject, that is a luxury that virtually none of us can afford.

5.1.4   Chatman's theories

In order to understand the meaning of these discussions in a broader context and in relation to transliterate academic cultures, a digression to overview the theories of Elfreda Chatman is required. Chatman developed her information theory about social aspects of information behavior in a series of studies of groups of people usually considered as information-poor—retired women, inmates of a women's prison, janitors, and women who practiced eating dirt for its perceived benefits. Chatman's studies showed that these groups had complex information practices. Chatman's research led to an information theory of a "small world" and a "life in the round," which showed how groups influence and determine information behavior.

The concept of a small world is included in a theory of "life in the round." Chatman (2000, p. 3) described the concept of a small world as "a world in which everyday happenings occur with some degree of predictability." "A small world is also defined by natural philosophy and everyday *knowledge*" (Chatman, 1999, p. 210). Social norms, worldview, social types, and information behavior are key concepts in her theory of normative behavior (Chatman, 2000, p. 11):

> Normative behaviour is that behaviour which is viewed by inhabitants of a social world as most appropriate for that particular context. Essentially driven by mores and norms, normative behaviour provides a predictable, routine, and manageable approach to everyday reality. Aspects of interest are those things which serve to legitimize and justify values, which embody social existence.
>
> *Chatman 2000, p. 13*

The horizons of people living in a small world are defined by social norms. "Insiders" are people who have greater understanding of social norms and are able to "establish standards for everyone else" (Chatman, 1999, p. 212). The norms are defined by "legitimized others" who have a degree of control of information. "Legitimized others" were described as

... people who share physical and/or conceptual space within a common landscape of cultural meaning. Within the contextual understanding of information behaviours, the legitimized others place narrow boundaries around the possibilities of these behaviours. In other words, legitimized others shape, change, or modify the information that enters a small world in light of a world-view.

Chatman, 2000, p. 3

The social roles and functioning of the group are performed as part of regular daily life. This everyday life is the basis for Chatman's theory of a life in the round:

A life in the round is a public form of life. It is a lifestyle with an enormous degree of imprecision. Yet, it is this inexactitude that provides an acceptable level of certainty. This way of life sets standards by which one constructs everyday meaning from reality. It is a "taken-for-granted," "business-as-usual" style of being.

Chatman, 1999, p. 207

Chatman described her theory of life in the round in six propositional statements (Chatman, 1999, p. 214):

- The concept of a small world is central to a life in the round because it "establishes legitimized others (primarily 'insiders') within that world who set boundaries on behavior"
- "Social norms force private behavior to undergo public scrutiny. It is this public arena that deems behavior—including information-seeking behavior—appropriate or not"
- "The result of establishing appropriate behavior is the creation of a worldview"
- "For most of us, a worldview is played out as life in the round," which is "a life taken for granted." Most of the time it is predictable enough that there is no need for information
- "Members who live in the round will not cross the boundaries of their world to seek information"
- Boundary crossing happens under certain conditions: "(1) the information is perceived as critical, (2) there is a collective expectation that the information is relevant, and (3) a perception exists that the life lived in the round is no longer functioning."
- Information has to be trusted and believable to be accepted. The most believable information conforms to common sense. Information is judged as credible because the provider is trusted and the source can be easily verified (Chatman, 1999, p. 215).

Withholding information or secrecy is an information behavior aiming at preserving one's autonomy and it is caused by social norms (Chatman, 1996). Chatman points out that the "primary issue has to do with information need and factors that *hinder* persons from making use of relevant knowledge that, in many cases, is not only public (that is, known) but also accessible" (p. 196). Chatman's definition of information poverty does not necessarily concern the amount of information that is available, but rather the way in which social norms limit the use of information:

When concerns and problems present themselves and when information is recognized as potentially helpful but is ignored, individuals live in an impoverished information world. Determined to hold the seams of their life-world together, they engage in self-protective behaviours, which define the finite boundaries of a world of poverty.

Chatman, 2000, p. 7

Chatman showed that powerful social rules determine conditions and ways in which information is sought, what acceptable information is, and what appropriate uses of information are. Individuals usually conform or keep socially unacceptable practices private.

5.1.5   Living in a city of villages

The theory of "living in a city of villages" is based on insights from the translit-eracy study and Chatman's theories. It explains how disciplines and academic insti-tutions determine social norms, group practices, and individual information behaviors in the process of academic boundary-crossing.

5.1.5.1   Academic small worlds

Chatman's theories were based on studies of the information behavior of groups of people usually considered as information-poor. Taken at face value, it is difficult to relate their information practices to those of academics, who constitute one of the most sophisticated groups of information users. However, Chatman's theory defines general principles applicable to any group whose life is defined by living in a small world. The strength of different disciplinary norms and traditions within academia is the reason for choosing the plural form in the expression "academic small worlds."

For scholars, their work is an integral part of their life. They spend long hours working from both home and office, and feel committed to their job. For aca-demics, work occupies a significant part of their life and often defines who they are. This sense of belonging and identity is one of the defining elements of a small world (Chatman, 1999). Scholars' "life in the round" is about work "as usual" when novelties such as new technology are gradually integrated into the way their small world operates.

Social types are central to the normative behavior of a social group (Chatman, 2000). "Legitimized others" are comparable with "big guns," described by Participant 5/2 as academics in positions of power. They need to be convinced that a piece of research can and should enter the academic circle. Like scholars' peers, Chatman's "insiders" are people who are in command of norms and they judge what is trivial or useless: "They are the quintessential frame of reference for observ-ing and controlling not only behavior, but also the information flow into a social world" (Chatman, 1999, p. 212). When the study participants talked about "stu-dents," "young generation," "traditional historians," "big guns," and "people who work in out there fields," they described academic social types that play a part in shaping information processes.

Secrecy and self-protective behaviors are part of living in a small world. Scholars choose to make their private information behaviors, such as the use of electronic sources, public in relation to the norms, worldviews and possible reactions of their peers who have roles of "insiders" and "legitimized others." An impoverished life's world is often related to self-protective behaviors. It does not relate to an absolute amount of information that has been shared but rather to an undisclosed information need. Self-protective behavior is apparent in situations when the need for information is recognized as potentially helpful but is ignored, often because of the desire to "appear normal" (Chatman, 2000, p. 7). The lack of discussion about uncertainties related to the use of electronic resources and the unexpressed need for training are signs of an impoverished life's world. The dismissive attitude of peers to the use of electronic resources is evident in scholars' public discourse, summarized in "all that crap from the net" as a conversation topic (U Participant 7/1). This discourse is quite likely to make an individual researcher reluctant to ask questions that would reveal the extent of her or his own use, which may be seen as unscholarly or unauthoritative. The majority of participants talked about an area where information about the use of e-texts was needed, but that information had not been sought.

Theories of a "small world" and "a life in the round" are interlinked, and Chatman's propositional statements that define the theory of a "life in the round" are related to the theory of a "small world." According to Chatman, the "result of establishing appropriate behavior is the creation of a worldview" (Chatman, 1999, p. 214). For academics, the discipline is the main arena that determines a world-view. Although academics may use different paradigms in their work and may exhibit different levels of unity in establishing common views and practices, there are worldviews shared within a disciplinary community.

Discussions in the study about perceived values of speed in research, for example, demonstrate the influence of disciplinary worldviews and attitudes. Traditional and electronic research were compared in developing hand-made products, and preparing slow- and fast-cooked food. Although the speed of electronic research, enabled by online interactions, was convenient and beneficial, there was an uneasy feeling that fast research was less valued. Participant 14/1 said that peers would not appreciate research based on e-resources, and Participant 2/1 thought that it might be viewed as "Mickey Mouse" or lazy. Participant 9/1 did not question the value of a fast study, but added: "I wouldn't like to say this too loudly because I think a lot of the scholars would consider that it was a shallow attitude." On the other hand, none of the scholars who worked in less traditional disciplines, such as media and communication studies, mentioned concerns about the speed of research and peers' perception of citations of e-texts. It seemed that this way of working was in line with dominant views in their fields.

Chatman's propositional statements of a "life in the round" say that participants who live in the round will not normally cross boundaries of a "small world" to seek information. When they do, it is because information is perceived as critical, there is a collective expectation that it is relevant, and there is a perception that a life in the round is no longer functioning (Chatman, 1999, p. 214). While these statements are still applicable to academics, they need to be elaborated and interpreted for academic contexts. Crossing boundaries will be considered in the framework of a "small world."

5.1.5.2 The academic city of villages

Academic disciplines define the norms and practices accepted by a disciplinary community and set the boundaries of academic small worlds. However, disciplines do not function as isolated environments. It is increasingly common that scholars work in interdisciplinary fields and belong to different disciplinary communities, negotiating their different cultures, traditions, and expectations. Many study participants negotiate traditions of different disciplines as well as creative and theoretical, or experimental and traditional academic work. Even if they remain within the boundaries of a single discipline, they live in a vibrant information environment populated by international scholars. This vibrant environment can be seen as an information metropolis. At the same time, academics follow the rules of their immediate disciplinary communities, which form their small worlds. "City of villages," a metaphor promoted by town planners of cities such as San Diego, Los Angeles, Dublin, and Sydney, is used here to present some of the dynamics of living in disciplinary "small worlds" or "villages" within an information metropolis.

Scholars usually have a primary discipline, but they seek information in other disciplines if that is the requirement of their projects. The boundary-crossing usually happens according to the rules of the primary discipline. For example, Participant 12/1 worked in a well-defined discipline where she has been a recognized expert. The researcher has normally used established electronic editions designed for specialists in the field. A sense of authority is based on knowing sources very well. However, to satisfy the requirements of a particular project, she had to leave the established information paths and seek information in other ways in neighboring fields. The process happened according to the dominant academic tradition by following the advice of a colleague in one of these other fields. In other words, the researcher does not normally leave her village in search of information, but when she has to do that, it happens according to the rules of following well-established academic expertise.

For other scholars, negotiation of different disciplinary rules is an important and complex aspect of presenting their scholarly work. When Participant 6/2 decided to write a book aiming at opening a dialog with very traditional scholars, he excluded references to all sources that he felt would not be acceptable to these colleagues. However, he introduced a style of writing promoted by interactions with electronic sources, which "pushed the edges" of traditional scholarship. Participant 1/1 negotiated the requirements of creative and academic writing in different ways without being quite sure about the established standard. Both researchers negotiated the rules of different villages where they spent significant time and which affected their work. In some instances, negotiation is very difficult. Participant 9/1 conducted nontraditional historical research, which included the use of unconventional sources viewed with suspicion in her discipline, and received contradictory peer reviews. Participant 7/1 conducted a wide search, including nonacademic sources, which was accepted in her discipline, but she had struggled with information overload.

In terms of living in a city of small villages, going to blogs, tourist websites, and discussion lists of people who believe in extraterrestrials meant leaving an academic neighborhood to roam around the city and listen to the stories in dark alleys and under the bridges. Stories from the underbelly of the city are often socially unacceptable in established disciplinary clubs in university quarters. Scholars who frequent the clubs, but cross the boundaries of academia, often learn from the "dark stories" and consider how to present them according to accepted disciplinary conventions. In nontraditional fields within traditional disciplines, it means more or less successful "dressing up" of research, which Participant 5/2 described as a way of using disciplinary theories and citations to make unconventional research acceptable to the mainstream discipline. In more traditional literary and historical studies, it means taking unaccepted sources into account without referring to them openly.

Scholars who do cross boundaries against the rules of their discipline would do so because information is perceived as critical or there is a perception that a life in the round is no longer functioning. Rapid changes in academia, inconsistent systems of promotions and evaluation of scholarly work, as well as conflicting expectations, indicate that the academic life is functioning with a number of difficulties. Contradictory influences were discussed by study participants as well. Participant 5/2 talked about a number of differences in circumstances, mentalities, and values between older and younger generations of researchers. Participant 15/1 talked about experimenting "without an umpire" in mind in the environment in which some peers are interested in experimental work with the multiplicity of resources, while others do not think that it meets scholarly standards. According to this participant, scholars who work in new fields start within a traditional discipline and gradually split away when another community takes shape.

In a metropolis, news travel fast and it is impossible to maintain local customs untouched, but that does not negate the existence and influence of small villages.

5.1.5.3   Authority

Social dimensions underpin issues of authority. First, the criteria for judging authority are socially constructed. Secondly, judgments on authority often motivate practical decisions such as the selection of information of good quality as well as information behaviors, such as secrecy and crossing the boundaries of small worlds. Thirdly, scholarly practices and a construction of the meaning of authority influence each other and any change can give an impetus to a shift in social norms.

Cognitive authority is a critical issue in an academic world. If e-texts were viewed as completely untrustworthy or unacceptable from the perspective of demonstrating one's cognitive authority, it is likely that they would be simply avoided. However, researchers often "trawl the net every day" (U Participant 14/1) and use e-resources throughout the research process, sometimes with significant investment in time and effort. The reason for the investment is that e-texts help them to do better research and, consequently, enhance their cognitive authority. If scholars were using only trustworthy scholarly texts, it would be easy to assume that these texts would gradually become as acceptable as any other traditional source. However, scholars use a range of nonacademic sources such as blogs, online discussions, and various websites, because these texts also help them to do better research and enhance their own cognitive authority.

Creativity and original thinking are often based on making connections between disparate ideas. The transliteracy study indicated that interactions with a wide variety of materials support thinking, and online practices made interactions with a variety of texts easier. However, scholars have always had an opportunity to investigate and learn from nonacademic sources. Academia has a long tradition of dealing with problems of acknowledging what is considered dispensable or unauthoritative. Nelson (2001) referred to Shotter's idea of "institutional forgetting" as a way of constructing a memory of a text. This process is relevant to building a reputation in academia and, eventually, histories of human thought. Forgetting becomes easier when originators of ideas have never been promoted to the full view of academia, particularly when the originators are women, and people of less powerful social, racial, and ethnic backgrounds. The resurrection of Foucault's subjugated knowledges may take the form of hardly visible undercurrents as long as power relations have a strong influence on knowledge claims, as argued by Lyotard (1984).

On the other hand, "and there is always 'the other hand' with the Web," as a study participant noted, maintaining monopolies and making "somebody a non-person" is increasingly difficult because of the multitude of possible sources (U Participant 10/1). As with a multitude of sources and academic styles, the notion of academic authority is becoming increasingly diverse. From references to groups of young scholars who follow online communication channels rather than official academic avenues, and interests in "linguistically subversive" texts to occasional disregard for traditional disciplines and authority—the study participants discussed subversive, or at least nontraditional, academic authority. "The path charted between the two poles of dialogue radically abolishes problems of causality, finality, etc., from our philosophical arena ... More than binarism, dialogism may well become the basis of our time's intellectual structure" (Kristeva, 1980, p. 89). The emergence of collaboration and collective construction of meaning disrupts reliance on individual authority. Dialogs also emerge from the juxtaposition of ideas from different knowledge strata. The question of what constitutes cognitive authority becomes then a matter of a dialog between different authorities, and the lack of the final answer becomes a sign of our time.

5.1.5.4   The historical moment

The changing academic tradition and the notion of authority happen in the context of wider changes in society, which have particular importance for research in the humanities. Historical and literary research is in a constant dialog with tradition, which is viewed from a context of contemporary people and their historical moments. When Participant 5/2 talked about historians' interests in contemporary topics, a different relationship between high and low culture and the different sensibility of the younger generation of researchers, and when Participant 13/1 discussed the significance of electronic searching in the context of the lack of trust in a single authority, they described societal changes which have had direct effects on research practices. The contemporary lack of trust and interest in traditional institutions and authorities contextualized some of the tensions between old and new scholarly approaches. When Participant 5/2 talked about "dressing up" modern historical studies to make them acceptable for "big guns" and to ensure the accreditation of younger scholars, she illustrated a way in which broader societal changes gradually influence academia. This is also the way in which a "life in the round" changes.

A number of changes in modern academia are related to ICTs, which have already had a visible impact on scholarship. It can be argued that electronic resources are not necessarily part of these observable changes, and that they can be adopted and incorporated in traditional scholarship without disturbing its structure. However, a number and a variety of small changes do affect overall structure and e-resources have already introduced a number of minor and significant changes in the way scholars go about regular work. Some of these changes are directly part of qualitative transformations of scholarship.

Gadamer wrote that the "idea that everything can be reversed, that there is always time for everything and that everything somehow returns, proves to be an illusion. Rather, the person who is situated and acts in history continually experiences the fact that nothing returns" (2004, p. 357). Participant 5/2 made a similar comment in relation to a broader context of academic changes in which we see a resurrection of conservatism and an apparent return to traditional values:

> *And I think that like the attempt to revitalise reasonably conservative kinds of religion, sometimes people will think that those sorts of conservative social values suit them for the moment, but when their life changes and they no longer want those conservative social values, i.e., they want to get a divorce or they decide that they're gay or whatever, it's changed now, you don't have to fear that anyone will disapprove of you if you want to get a divorce or you want to form a same sex partnership. So you can't turn back the clock.*

Chatman's observation that changes come to a small stage first (Chatman, 1999) is particularly acute from the perspective of the humanities as one of the oldest academic fields, defined by a dialog with tradition. There were times when revolutionary changes seemed to be on the main stage of the discipline, but it was only for a short time. This small world can be transformed only through evolution, although it is important to remember that we are living in a historical moment marked by relatively fast changes. Even evolution has become faster.

5.2 Transliteracy in the hybrid world

The academic city of villages is situated in the world characterized by boundary-crossing and global movements. If some of the disciplinary and traditional academic boundaries are becoming arbitrary and then reinforced with renewed agility, similar processes are happening on state, national, and cultural levels. Globalization has captured the interest and imagination of people, governments, and various academic disciplines around the world. Some argue that it is not a real phenomenon, at least not more significant than other global trends have been in history. However, the prominence of globalization in contemporary thinking and imagination deserves some attention, since transliteracy as a literacy of "moving across" is situated in the broad context of global trends. In this section, a brief detour will be made to consider globalization and set a backdrop for further discussion about the idea of hybrids and hybrid cultures in which transliteracy finds its relevant social context.

5.2.1 Global, national, regional

Globalization has been considered in some way by most social sciences, with many disagreements about the existence and nature of the change. Nederveen Pieterse (2015) wrote a comprehensive review of prominent discussions and found that, amid all the disputes, there is the core of agreement:

> . . .globalization is being shaped by technological changes, involves the reconfiguration of states, goes together with regionalization, and is uneven. Another common understanding, that globalization means time-space compression, may be vague enough not to cause much stir. It means that globalization involves more intensive interaction across wider space and in shorter time than before, in other words, the experience of a shrinking world; yet this may also be too simple and flat an account [p. 17].

A significant part of the process is the change in the role of nation states, which were the main form of political organization from the mid 19th to the mid 20th century, when regionalization became a prominent force, with the European Union as the prime example (Nederveen Pieterse, 2015). At the same time, citizens of the developing countries migrated to the centers of former imperial power in large numbers (Tomlinson, 2013). During the last several decades, many states have also changed their borders and names, and often shaped new identities.

While political boundaries are shifting, cultural differences are increasingly being formed around ethnic, religious, regional, race, gender, and minority identities. The cultural shifts may appear less significant than political and economic changes associated with global movements, but culture "is general human software—and none of the world's hard enterprises functions without software. Desires and goals, and methods and expectations in achieving goals, are all of a cultural nature. Power itself is a cultural dream" (Nederveen Pieterse, 2015, p. 131).

Understanding of the meaning of cultural differences as part of globalization is viewed as comprising three significantly different perspectives, described as paradigms by Nederveen Pieterese. This author identifies three paradigms: "clash of civilizations," McDonaldization, and hybridization. The view of lasting cultural differences was articulated by Samuel Huntington as the "clash of civilizations," according to which significant cultural differences make civilizations profoundly at odds with each other. This perspective puts in focus differences without accounting for many "in-between" cultural forms:

> Intercultural diffusion through trade and migration, a lingua franca between cultures, returnees from abroad with bicultural experience, children of mixed

parentage, travelers with multicultural experience, professionals interacting
cross-culturally, the fields of cyberspace—all of these fall outside 'culture'.
Nederveen Pieterse, 2015, p. 46

McDonaldization, as a shortcut for many other expressions with the "Mc" prefix, signifies the idea that societies are becoming homogenized through the impact of multinational corporations and their interests. This paradigm explains convergence toward the most powerful countries and multinational groups. What it does not explain are many instances of the changing of global products for the local market. As Nederveen Pieterse pointed out, Russian McDonald's is a very different fast food chain from the original company. Neither of the two paradigms responds to the following challenge:

How do we come to terms with phenomena such as Thai boxing by Moroccan girls
in Amsterdam, Asian rap in London, Irish bagels, Chinese tacos, and Mardi Gras
Indians in the United States, or 'Mexican schoolgirls dressed in Greek togas
dancing in the style of Isadora Duncan' [Rowe and Schelling, 1991, p. 161]?
    How do we interpret Peter Brook directing the Mahabharata, or Ariane
Mnouchkine staging a Shakespeare play in Japanese Kabuki style for a Paris
audience in the Théâtre Soleil?
Nederveen Pieterse, 2015, p. 65.

These questions are not only important in explaining the nature of globalization, but they concern the essence of transliteracy. This is why the third approach to global cultures will be considered in some detail.

5.2.2   Hybridization

Mixing, borrowing, transitioning, changing have been the way cultures have developed from the beginning. Well before the existence of the modern states, people, objects, and ideas traveled across tribal, territorial, and cultural boundaries. In that sense, globalization and hybridization are nothing new. What is new is the nature and extent of hybridization, which impacts a sense of cultural identities. The nature of changes, which contracts space and time, emphasizes what Serveas and Lie (2003) described as the view of cultural identity as a process rather than a finished product. Similarly, Hannerz (1987, p. 550) points out a "management of meaning" involved in the cultural "work in progress" in which "cultures can perhaps never be completely worked out as stable, coherent systems." Nederveen Pieterse (2015, p. 131) considered the origin of the nation state and asked whether a sense of cultural identity should revolve around a sedentary rather than a mobile point of view. The nation state "... grew out of sedentary experiences, agriculture, urbanism, and then industry as anchors of the national economy. The nation state inherited older territorial imperatives, and 'national interest' translated them into geopolitical and geostrategic niches and projects. Together they make up a real estate vision of history."

The key for the understanding of hybridity is in the nature of boundaries and their crossing, as was the case in considering academic cultures. Power relations have been well recognized in this field. Tomlinson (2013, p. 145) pointed out that "the metaphors of mixing and confluence tend to suggest 'equal measures' and a certain serendipity in the combination... But the sceptical position points precisely to the unequal balance in the cultural resources that are engaged and to the familiar established hegemonies."

The inequality embedded in hybridization has profound implications for the knowledge field. While the stance of openness is desirable as it enables enrichment and growth, in both the cultural and the economic sense, affirmation of some boundaries or protective measures may be necessary to ensure cultural diversity. Faced by the dominance of Western cultural content through media, some Asian countries decided to introduce protectionist measures to shield their own cultural values and ensure the development of local creative content. The argument that with globalization there may be less difference between localities, but more variety within them goes only halfway in understanding the pattern of diversity. McDonaldization as a paradigm does not provide a comprehensive perspective, but issues of homogenization cannot be ignored either. European fashion labels, for example, may include design elements from Asia and Latin America, introducing exotic visual elements in shops across Europe. The shop appearance and status can vary as well as the way the clothes are presented on streets. However, the dominance of the label and its marketing ensure that the pattern of variety is similar across the globe. The loss of unique local crafts and the struggle of small local businesses in the face of competition with multinational companies are real.

In the field of hybridity, contradictions are everywhere. While cultural openness is promoted, cultural diversity may be threatened at the same time. Protectionism also has many disguises. If we learned anything from thinking about transliteracy, it is that there is always the climate, the hand, the language of the local.

5.2.3   Transliterate boundary-crossing

By its nature, transliteracy is mobile, nomadic, and hybrid. By definition, it is situated in the knowledge, social, and cultural fields in which it is a literacy of "moving across." Since knowledge, society, culture, and particularly "boundary-crossing," are never politically neutral, transliterate reflection must be political on one level. A difficult question is what is involved in the politics of boundary-crossing. Is it conducive to transliterate ways of knowing to keep the gates open? Or, to close them and ensure mixing and merging of what was selected to stay in?

5.2.3.1   The case for opening

The transliteracy study shows the benefits of access to all sorts of materials. Scholars have always encountered a variety of resources in all formats during the research process, but electronic resources and interactions have a prominent role in bringing together a wide variety of texts, many of them nonacademic. Texts from mailing lists and bulletin boards that discuss gossip and stories about historical personalities correspond to Bakhtin's Menippean discourse. Researchers in the study discussed how interactions with unauthoritative e-texts contributed to their understanding of the topic and influenced the inclusion of a multiplicity of voices into scholarly writing. In Menippean discourse, "[a]cademic problems are pushed aside in favor of the 'ultimate' problems of existence: this discourse orients liberated language towards philosophical universalism" (Kristeva, 1980, pp. 82−83). Historians who want to explore contemporary phenomena, who are interested in any voice that can contribute to their understanding of a topic, which they see as a real-life rather than a purely academic issue, are open to Menippean discourse. Scholars' use of historical methods to investigate topics such as the religion of Jediisim contribute to Menippean discourse by investigating texts "from the underworld" and introducing them sometimes directly, but more often indirectly to academic writing. Like Menippean discourse, which is "a kind of political journalism of its time" (Kristeva, 1980, p. 83), these academic dialog with unconventional texts document some contemporary tensions and become part of daily conversations. Multimedia and traditional academic works both contribute to the cycle of "spinning" the knowledge to the benefit of the whole society.

In parallel with the digital culture of opening is the politics of representation and access, which brings the power of corporate and government gatekeepers into play. While on the one hand, many more government and historical documents are within easy reach than ever before, on the other, access control has been revised in the light of online data sharing, increased concerns about protection of privacy, rights of minorities and possible compensation claims, to name just a few. For example, the concept of Stolen Generations (forcible removal of Indigenous children from their families) is a well-recognized part of Australian history, based on historical investigations and government inquiry (Australian Human Rights Commission, 1997; Australian Government, 2015b). Historian and study participant, Peter Read, who had a pivotal role in bringing the historical findings into public consciousness, wrote the following about the contemporary access restrictions to archival documents, which led to the discovery of Stolen Generations:

Mental health records are closed by [sic! Australian] governments for 100 years unless permission is obtained by all parties. There is an obvious reason for this, but arguably all older archives should be open. Permission granted to responsible researchers working with sensitive materials who have signed the appropriate protocols, covers most other archives which fall outside the "thirty-year rule."

A further justification for keeping the archives open is to allow historians to see the whole government view of mental health, or anything else.

In 1980 I received permission from the New South Wales Department of Youth and Community Services to read all of the archives relating to the Aborigines Welfare and Aborigines Protection Boards. This enabled me to "discover" the story of the Stolen Generation, though scattered through some 20,000 other records: hundreds of heart-breaking personal files, minutes of meetings, general correspondence, the child separation policy displayed in all its intentions, practice and effects.

*I obtained permission because no official had any idea what the Aboriginal
archives contained. Six months later, when my pamphlet "The Stolen Generations"
passionately revealed what I had read, the NSW government supported the
publication, and still does; but little by little, departments in all states began to
realise the risks of letting researchers loose in archives whose content was
unknown [the Commonwealth Archives have always been much more careful].
Today very many archives that mention individuals are closed.*

*I believe that I was the first and last non-government employee to read these
records. To close up our history in this way is a tragedy for our national
understanding.*

Read, 2016

It is Derrida's archive fever burning at the closed doors. A number of both academics and students in the transliteracy study noted that a great deal of quality resources are protected by copyright or access restriction. Regardless of the reasons for restrictions, they are viewed by study participants as, often unnecessary, obstacles. Discussions about governments and corporations, which hold abundant data about citizens while making sure their information is well protected, have a place in conversations about imposed boundaries.

5.2.3.2   The case for protection

An understanding of cultural richness is at the core of the humanities work and this is why humanists need access to sources from all historical periods, to all editions, variations, and materials of different provenance. By the same token, transliteracy benefits from mixing and merging, and also from the preservation of various stages of cultural transition. The claim that every culture is a hybrid and none is pure is not an argument against protection and preservation. In order to understand evolution, sciences need fossils from various stages of this development, and in order to understand our ability to produce music, remote folk music, and notes from a distant past are immensely beneficial, not to mention their stimulation of creativity.

Preservation is particularly important for protection of endangered cultural heritage and a sense of cultural ownership. Access to records about Australian Indigenous people and their culture can, once again, serve as an example, this time for a protectionist stance. Australian Indigenous cultures are the oldest surviving cultures on earth (Australian Government, 2015a). It is likely that they were exposed to other influences, but compared with all other current cultures, they present the purest living cultural form. Not only does this require protection in the same way as all other Indigenous cultures, its unique cultural value warrants close scrutiny in protecting this heritage. The current position in the Australian library and information sector, developed in cooperation with the Indigenous communities, is to preserve Aboriginal cultural artifacts and knowledge in a culturally sensitive way, even if it means restricted access (Nakata and Langton, 2005). This is, on one hand, an acknowledgment of different traditions in knowledge management, on another, an attempt to protect the copyright and moral rights of Indigenous communities. Although real-life practices are many and varied, there is at least agreement among cultural and knowledge institutions on what is required to protect and preserve Australian Indigenous cultures.

Preservation can go hand in hand with creativity and knowledge growth. Indigenous artists combine modern sensibilities with ancient techniques to produce innovative creations. Indigenous knowledge of plants and healing has been applied to enrich Western medicine and Aboriginal fire control methods have found their place in official procedures. Without considering many social and cultural complexities, suffice to say that both the preservation and the cross-fertilization surrounding Indigenous cultures are immersed in controversies and power struggles, but at least there is a base of shared understanding of what constitutes a desired approach, with protection being of the utmost importance.

5.2.3.3 Transliterate boundary-crossing

Opening up, crossing over, combining into hybrid things what used to be remote and separate is exciting and enriching, but the connection with the local and traditional is never completely lost. A view that migration, globalization, and cultural diffusion via the Internet are a threat to the tribal and regional is relevant in this context (Akhtar, 2005). Trends toward globalization can be compared with trends to merging boundaries between disciplines, scholarly and unscholarly sources, theoretical and creative writing, which are supported by working online. Fundamentalism as an opposing trend, discussed by Akhtar, has limited parallels with what is happening in schools and universities as discussed in this book, but it still indicates a force in maintaining traditional disciplinary boundaries and values. Electronic sources are hybrids, which enable intertextuality and fast movement across time and space, which promise to bring together what is separate, and open boundaries, but also threaten to destroy the order and traditions of small worlds. A psychiatrist, Akhtar (2005, p. 128), considered the emotional effect of hybrid things: "It captures what is the most pure, wide-eyed, and childlike in us. It says that elements that seemed incompatible can actually be combined to beneficial effect. It reminds us that more is possible and that the constituents of novelty are at our disposal all the time." It is not accidental that the opposite is emerging at the same time as migration, globalization, and cultural fusions enabled by technology are becoming a prominent part of our lives:

> And, as a recoil to this development, each is manifesting the resurgence of orthodoxy and regressive search for purity. No wonder polarized camps of hybridization and fundamentalism have sprung up everywhere. One can only hope that the synthesis of these diverse ideologies might yield pathways toward a future that is based upon the present and is not entirely divorced from the past. Donald Winnicott's celebrated phrase "There is no originality except on the basis of tradition" comes to mind in this context.
>
> Akhtar, 2005, p. 135

Transliteracy is a literacy of hybridity. It is a mindset which holds the understanding that there is a time and place for separation, for mindful cross-fertilization, and for abundant merging and mixing. It holds the understanding that disciplines, single crafts, unique techniques, and special knowledges need to be separate at times in the same way that we as individuals need time to be private and alone. It includes not only the culture of respectful sharing and skills for collaboration, but also sharp critical thinking and a political mind for living in the global village. It is a cultivated and educated mindset. Crossing boundaries is a tricky business, which needs to be taught, learned, thought through, improvised, and practiced. Transliteracy implies a challenge—to one's own skills and thinking, and to an established order. Practiced at its heights, it is a breath-taking walk on a tightrope, which has something new to reveal about our own limits.

5.3 Summary

In this chapter, transliteracy was considered in the context of academic and broader hybrid cultures. In the first part, "Academic cultures and transliteracy," authority and authenticity, changes in research, and scholarly communities were discussed in relation to the evidence from the study of transliteracy and broader literature. A theory of "living in a city of villages" was presented on the basis of Elfreda Chatman's theories. Academic "small worlds" and a "city of villages" were introduced as concepts to explain information exchanges and boundary-crossing in academia.

The second part, "Transliteracy in the hybrid world," considered globalization as a background for further discussions about hybrid cultures in which transliteracy is situated. Issues of information and cultural protection and opening were illustrated by examples of Australian experience in dealing with Indigenous history and culture. The chapter points toward a need to cultivate transliteracy as a set of skills and behaviors, suitable for changeable and complex contexts.

References

Akhtar, S., 2005. Objects of Our Desire: Exploring Our Intimate Connections with the Things Around Us. Harmony Books, New York.

Andersen, D.L., Trinkle, D.A., 2004. Valuing digital scholarship in the tenure, promotion, and review process. In: Andersen, D.L. (Ed.), Digital Scholarship in the Tenure, Promotion, and Review Process. M.E. Sharpe, Armonk, NY.

Andersen, D.L. (Ed.), 2004. Digital Scholarship in the Tenure, Promotion, and Review Process. M.E. Sharpe, Armonk, NY.

Australian Government, 2015a. Australian Indigenous Cultural Heritage.Digital Transformation Office, Canberra. Available from: http://www.australia.gov.au/about-australia/australian-story/austn-indigenous-cultural-heritage (accessed 17.06.16).

Australian Government, 2015b. Sorry Day and the Stolen Generations.Digital Transformation Office, Canberra. Available from: http://www.australia.gov.au/about-australia/australian-story/sorry-day-stolen-generations (accessed 17.06.16).

Australian Human Rights Commission, 1997. Bringing them home: The 'Stolen Children' report.

Becher, T., 1989. Academic Tribes and Territories. The Society for Research into Higher Education, Milton Keynes.

Belkin, N.J., 1994. Design principles for electronic textual resources: investigating users and uses of scholarly information. In: Zampolli, A., Calzolari, N., Palmer, M. (Eds.), Current Issues in Computational Linguistics. Giardini, Pisa.

Bolter, J.D., 2001. Writing Space: Computers, Hypertext, and the Remediation of Print. Lawrence Erlbaum Associates, Mahwah, NJ.

Brown, J.S., Duguid, P., 1996. The social life of documents. First Monday, 1.

Buckland, M.K., 1991. Information and Information Systems. Greenwood Press, New York.

Burgess, H.J., Hamming, J., 2011. New media in the academy: labor and the production of knowledge in scholarly multimedia. Digital Humanities Quarterly, 5. Available from: http://www.digitalhumanities.org/dhq/vol/5/3/000102/000102.html.

Burnett, K., Mckinley, G.E., 1998. Modelling information seeking. Interact Comp. 10, 285−302.

Chatman, E.A., 1996. The impoverished life-world of outsiders. J. Am. Soc. Inform. Sci. 47, 193−206.

Chatman, E.A., 1999. A theory of life in the round. J. Am. Soc. Inform. Sci. 50, 207−217.

Chatman, E.A., 2000. Framing social life in theory and research. New Rev. Inform. Behav. Res. 1, 3−17.

Derrida, J., 1996. Archive Fever: a Freudian Impression. University of Chicago Press, Chicago.

DLF, 2004. DLF's scholars panel. DLF Quarterly Update: July 1−September 30, 2004. Digital Library Federation.

Foucault, M., 1980. Two lectures. In: Gordon, C. (Ed.), Power-Knowledge: Selected Interviews and Other Writings, 1972−1977. Harvester, New York.

Gadamer, H.-G., 2004. Truth and Method. Continuum, New York.

Hannerz, U., 1987. The world in creolisation. Africa 57, 546−559.

Haraway, D., 1992. The promises of monsters: a regenerative politics for inappropriate/d others. In: Grossberg, L., Treichler, P.A., Nelson, C. (Eds.), Cultural Studies. Routledge, New York.

Kristeva, J., 1980. Word, dialogue, and novel. In: Roudiez, L.S. (Ed.), Desire in Language: a Semiotic Approach to Literature and Art. Columbia University Press, New York.

Lyotard, J.-F., 1984. The Postmodern Condition: a Report on Knowledge. Manchester University Press, Manchester.

Mcgann, J., 1998. Textual scholarship, textual theory, and the uses of electronic tools: a brief report on current undertakings. Victor. Stud. 41, 609−619.

Nakata, M., Langton, M. (Eds.), 2005. Australian Indigenous Knowledge and Libraries. UTS ePress.

Nederveen Pieterse, J., 2015. Globalization and culture: global mélange, Globalization. 3rd ed. Rowman & Littlefield Publishers, Lanham.

Nelson, N., 2001. Discourse synthesis: the process and the product. In: Mcinnis, R.G. (Ed.), Discourse Synthesis: Studies in Historical and Contemporary Social Epistemology. Praeger, Westport, CT.

Neumann, L.J., 2001. Communities of practice as information systems: humanities scholars and information convergence. PhD diss., University of Illinois at Urbana-Champaign.

Read, P., 2016. RE: Access to Australian archival records. Type to SUKOVIC, S.

Rowe, W., Schelling, V., 1991. Memory and Modernity: Popular Culture in Latin America, London.
Serveas, J., Lie, R., 2003. Media, globalisation and culture: issues and trends. Communication. 29, 7–23.
Sukovic, S., 2008. Information discovery in ambiguous zones of research. Librar. Trends. 57, 72–87.
Sukovic, S., 2009. References to e-texts in academic publications. J. Document. 65, 997–1015.
Taylor, R.S., 1991. Information use environments. In: Dervin, B., Voigt, M.J. (Eds.), Progress in Communication Sciences. ABLEX, Norwood, NJ.
Tomlinson, J., 2013. Globalization and Culture. Wiley, Hoboken.
Wilson, P., 1983. Second-hand knowledge: an inquiry into cognitive authority. Greenwood Press, Westport, CT.

Implications for the library and information field

6

Most library and information professionals knew something about transliteracy before reading this book, even if they had never heard the term before. In some way, transliteracy is bound to be part of library and information practice. Understanding that it is an essential part of how our clients work with information, learn, and create knowledge is the next step and so is a commitment to transliterate ways of working. In the last chapter of this book, I will suggest a few ideas for thinking how to provide transliterate services and how to become transliterate professionals or academics. It is by no means an exhaustive account, more an attempt to provide some food for thought.

6.1 Transliterate services

A few years ago, I was involved in several projects around the *Library of the Future* initiative at the University of Technology, Sydney Library, when we investigated how staff see the future of their work and how young high school students (aged approximately 13−16), our future clients, want to work. It was a bit of a surprise that there was not much difference in the way these two groups saw the future of knowledge work and library development (Sukovic, 2011; Sukovic et al., 2011). Another moment of wonder was when I read the views of the "clients of the future" after finishing my work on the transliteracy study and discovered how closely aligned is the vision of the library of the future with findings about transliteracy. On second thought, there was no place for surprise, just a confirmation of the transliteracy study results.

Because of the implications for information services and because of a close alignment with transliteracy, I would like to revisit views of the clients of the future. The excerpt below is based on an article with my colleagues, David Litting and Ashley England (2011).

> *Open, flexible, green are the key words describing the students' vision for the future library. They want to work in flexible ways with multiple technologies in digital and physical environments which 'fire their imagination' and are sustainable.*
> *They expressed views demonstrating a strong global orientation and preference for open engagement. They want to work with a variety of people across the globe, to enable creation of content in different languages and listen to interesting stories of people with unusual experiences, such as refugees. At the same time, they are aware of the significance of a local place. In their description of a global magazine, they wanted headquarters to be in Australia because it 'has to lead in more things'.*

Transliteracy in Complex Information Environments. DOI: http://dx.doi.org/10.1016/B978-0-08-100875-1.00006-6

They want to work responsibly and ethically with minimal control and regulation with flexible work arrangements, including working at times that suit them, from home, office and any place where research is conducted. Students enjoy working in virtual and physical spaces and expect to have access to multiple physical and digital objects and formats.

Flexibility and remote collaboration are important, but they cannot replace direct communication with people. This is an important reason why physical spaces are still relevant. Libraries and offices should be stimulating pleasant spaces with unusual objects and artwork to provide room for quiet individual work as well as for group work, socializing and relaxation. The inviting work space is 'random', meaning surprising, different from predictable monotonous environments, where a person wants to stay and work. There is a strong preference for spaces which bring the outside space inside by having lots of plants, water features, courtyards, and windows or transparent walls with views. Students wish to work by engaging all senses and prefer spaces and materials which support multisensory experiences.

Technology is important to students as easily used tools which support their work. Students like the use and visibility of technology, but only as much as it is functional and able to extend their work or experiences. They did not express preference for any particular technology with an implied understanding that any technology will be replaced by something new. They like flexible mobile technology which can be used wherever they are. For example, independent work in the field with a regular contact with the office is desirable as well as technology appearing anywhere where people spend time [a computer screen on toilet doors for reading was mentioned as an example]. Students want the content to be highly customizable and suggested the use of burstable balloons filled with ideas or suggestions where information can be found. Searching is particularly important and students want to be able to define what and how to search. Their preference for augmented reality relates to their preference for multi-sensory and real-life experiences.

In other words, students want to work in transliterate ways. They have a strong sense of place and the experiential, multisensory, and creative side of their information work. They value technology, but they know that technologies come and go. Their main requirement is that technologies mold into the way they work. They also need a connection with an "office," a place that will provide remote support and physical space. Students have a strong global consciousness and a desire to be connected with the world and also a sense of their national contribution. It is all good news for the libraries and information centers because our face-to-face and remote services are needed not only to assist people in dealing with a multiplicity of sources, information searching, and technology, but also to provide connection with a community.

Our clients want to paint their transliterate picture and need our support. My little fantasy is a *drag and drop library*—a bare room with writable walls and big screens, into which clients can "drag and drop" a few mobile furniture pieces, books, and any materials and technology they may be need. They can "order" a librarian (an information specialist, really, and probably in the plural, but let's call this person a "librarian") in this room who would help them with constructing a digital and physical corner for their work, and attend physically and remotely to assist with information. The librarian will be able to tinker with information and technology, and also to think big and see connections where no one else sees them.

In working with academics, the librarian is an information broker going between academic villages and enabling information transfer. With disciplinary and information knowledge, the librarian understands information environments and helps academics, not only in bringing the most relevant pieces of information, but also in pointing towards possible directions in implementing technology to aid research and in communicating information to reach outside the disciplinary village. With library buildings, collections, and online guides, librarians provide big structures, but they also understand the local and hands-on part of the work and provide services on both levels.

6.2 Transliterate professional or academic

At the beginning of this book, transliteracy was placed in the space between theory and practice. Transliteracy cannot be anything but a holistic process involving different types of knowledge. It has already been raised that one of the major obstacles to the inclusion of transliteracy in education is the existence of significant difficulties in going across subject and disciplinary divides, and also divisions between analytical and creative thinking. If the same argument is applied to the library and information field, divisions between different types of information expertise, and between theoretical and practical knowledge, appear equally obstructive. It is not only that they do not support transliteracy, they are counterproductive in understanding information as a whole.

Library and information science is an applied knowledge field. While purely theoretical investigations have their place, the field itself is positioned between theory and practice. Proponents of medical theory and practice understand this position very well, so medicine has a whole range of structures to ensure that academic research is grounded in the reality of work with patients. Following the idea of a "teaching hospital," I proposed that it is time to think about the "teaching library," with implications for librarian skill sets, organization of library and academic work, and career paths (Sukovic, 2015). Research grounded in practice, with strong connections between library and academic work, is a key aspect of this proposition. Transliteracy, as well as the rest of library and information studies, would benefit enormously from ongoing data-gathering in practice.

Insights into transliteracy, trends towards embedding technologies in the environment, the reality of lifelong learning and preparedness for job flexibility, all indicate that transliterate ways of working with information are here to stay and, quite likely, become more prominent in the future. Transliteracy provides a conceptual framework for thinking about the change. Technologies and specific literacies will come and go. As a profession, we have to know them to perform our duties, but each one can be replaced with the next thing as long as our focus is on our and our clients' ability to work with the variety and across the knowledge field.

Online environments have brought to the fore the fact that information has always had social and ideological underpinnings. As information and knowledge are becoming key contributors to the economy, and fast and multifarious information sharing central to the functioning of democracy, the information field has become a hotly contested territory. Librarians bring into this arena their reputation for trustworthiness and reliability. By continuing to work on enabling access to multiplicity of information and maintaining the professional ethos, libraries are likely to maintain their status, and also to be required to defend and assert their position. Transliteracy brings into focus not only the awareness that boundaries are part of social contexts, but also that boundary-crossing is a social activity with many participants. Political acumen and literacy for cultural hybridity are and will be highly valuable.

As the wishes of our clients of the future, shown above, demonstrate many young people have keen global and local consciousness. They want to live mindfully in the local place and participate in the global arena. They need nothing less than the whole society to make that possible. Transliteracy is concrete, hands-on, and practical, but it is also abstract and global. Transliteracy, with its high objective, is broad and ambitious in scope, but so is the information and knowledge field in which it is situated. Transliteracy is concerned with trajectories across this territory. Information and knowledge workers are its custodians and travel agents.

6.3 Summary

The last chapter considered implications of transliteracy for library and information work. Transliteracy is closely aligned with ideas about the flexible contemporary library, which supports clients' information practices in their variety. Information professionals have an important role to play as information brokers who can aid information transfer and cross-disciplinary work. Connections between library and information work in academia and in practice were presented as necessary for transliteracy and helpful for the field as a whole.

References

Sukovic, S., 2011. Strategically creative: a case of the library planning process. J. Organ. Transform. Social Change, 8.
Sukovic, S., 2015. Towards a teaching library: connecting academia and the profession. 8th International Evidence Based Library and Information Practice Conference (EBLIP8). Queensland University of Technology, Brisbane.
Sukovic, S., Litting, D., England, A., 2011. Playing with the future: library engagement and change. Austral. Acad. Res. Librar. 42, 70–87.

Index

Sources, 63–64. *See also* Topics
of research, 125
Stolen Generations, 145–146
Stordy, P., 3
Strauss, A., 15
St. Vincent's College, Sydney, 13–14
classroom learning, 101–102
curriculum mapping, 93*b*
Subjugated knowledges, 139–140
Survey Monkey, 22

T
Teaching library, 153
Team teaching, 102
Technology, 1
analog, 1–2
digital. *See Digital specific entries*
issues with, 58
and protocols, 58–60
Teenager, 108
Televised programs, 31
Textual studies, 119
Theory of living in a city of villages.
See Living in a city of villages
Third World, 142
Thomas, Sue, 6–7
Time and space, 81
Timing, classroom pedagogies, 102
Tomlinson, J., 144
Tools, classroom pedagogies, 102–103
Topics, 63–64. *See also* Sources
of research, 125
Traditional academic resources, 34
Transliteracy, 2
concept, 6–7
conceptual model, 29–31, 30*f*
constitutes, 31–52
creativity and, 8
culture and. *See* Academic cultures
key aspect of, 7
librarians and, 7
origins and development, 6–8
pedagogies for. *See* Pedagogies
working
with others, 40–45, 41*f*
with resources, 33–40, 33*f*
Transliteracy: Crossing Divides (Thomas),
6–7

Transliteracy palettes, 87–89
form palette, 88–89, 89*f*
information palette, 87–88, 87*f*
Transliteracy Project (Liu), 6
Transliteracy Research Group Archive,
7–8
Transliterate, 6
explorations, 37–40
reading and writing, 103–113
services, 151–153
Triangulation, 15, 23
Truth and Method (Gadamer), 14
Truth and Reality, 19
TV sets, 31
Tyner, K., 3

U
UNESCO, 2
United Kingdom, 105
University of Bordeaux, 8
University of California, 6
University of Sydney, 13
University of Technology, Sydney, 151
University setting, data gathering in, 20–21,
20*t*
electronic texts in humanities, 20–21
Indigenous history in Sydney, 21
participants' profile, 20*t*

V
Validity
descriptive, 24–25
interpretive, 25
Maxwell's approach to, 25
Video interviews, 37–38
Visual aspects of online content, 123

W
Wang, C.-L., 91–92
Working with others, 40–45, 41*f*
collaboration and cooperation, 41–43
communication, 43–44
netchaining, 44–45
Working with resources, 33–40, 33*f*
information retrieval, 35
multiplicity, 34–35
purpose, 35–37

Printed in the United States
By Bookmasters